✔ KU-285-617

16-19 MATHEMATICS

Modelling with differential equations

The School Mathematics Project

Tynemouth College
Queen Alexandra Road West
North Shields NE29 9BZ

CAMBRIDGE
UNIVERSITY PRESS

Main authors   Ann Kitchen
                      Kevin Lord
                      Mike Savage
                      Nigel Webb
                      Julian Williams

Team leaders   Kevin Lord and Julian Williams

Project director Stan Dolan

The authors would like to give special thanks to Ann White for her help in preparing this book for publication.

The publishers would like to thank the following for supplying photographs:

page 15 – Steve Crabtree
page 35 – NASA, Houston, USA
page 51 – NASA, Houston, USA
page 67 – Mechanics in Action Project

Cartoons by Paul Holland

Tynemouth College
Queen Alexandra Road West
North Shields NE29 9BZ

Published by the Press Syndicate of the University of Cambridge
The Pitt Building, Trumpington Street, Cambridge CB2 1RP
40 West 20th Street, New York, NY 10011-4211, USA
10 Stamford Road, Oakleigh, Victoria 3166, Australia

© Cambridge University Press 1993

First published 1993

Produced by 16-19 Mathematics and Laserwords, Southampton

Printed in Great Britain by Scotprint Ltd., Musselburgh.

ISBN 0 521 42642 1

Contents

1 *Modelling resisted motion*

1.1 Introduction

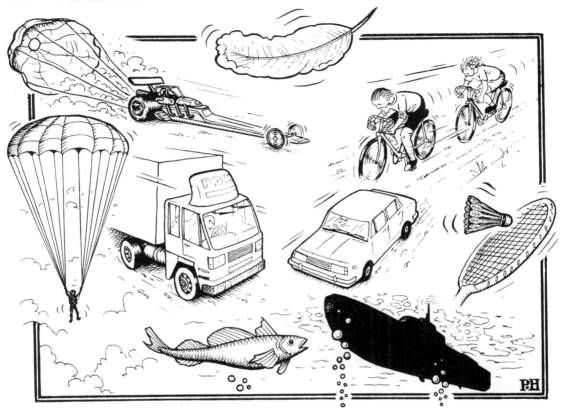

Situations like those shown above can be modelled using Newton's laws of motion. In previous units, you generally assumed the resistance force to be negligible (i.e. to be zero). This led to equations of motion that were relatively straightforward to solve. However, in some cases the resistance force, **drag**, cannot be ignored.

> **(a)**   **In what situations can resistance be used to advantage?**
>
> **(b)**   **What can be done to minimise the drag in cases where it is undesirable?**

In this unit you will be looking at the effects of introducing resistance and other variable forces into the model, at how this changes the equation of motion, and at the new methods needed to solve the resulting equation of motion.

1.2   Resistance to motion

> **(a)** Try dropping a ball of paper and a sheet of paper at the same time. Which falls faster? Account for your observations.
>
> **(b)** Imagine holding your hand out of the window of a moving car. Describe what it would feel like.
>
> **(c)** What is the force resisting motion in each of (a) and (b)?
>
> **(d)** What two factors seem to affect the magnitude of this force?

In order to analyse the motion of some objects, you need to develop a suitable model for air resistance. However, to do this you need a better understanding of the factors which affect the magnitude of the force.

TASKSHEET 1 – *Sky-diving*

Sophisticated experiments have been performed on smooth spheres positioned in a wind tunnel. The air is blown past them, and the resistance is measured.

It has been found that the force due to air resistance, R, can be modelled by an expression of the type:

$$A \; f(v)$$

where A is the cross-sectional surface area of the object perpendicular to the direction of motion and $f(v)$ is an increasing function of the speed v of the object through the air.

In many situations, the area for a particular object can be considered as constant, so that resistance can be modelled simply as a function of speed.

Although there is no simple formula relating the force, R, to speed, experiments suggest that two models are reasonable.

   $R = Kv$ is a suitable model for the air resistance at 'low' speeds,
   $R = kv^2$ is a suitable model for the air resistance at 'high' speeds,

where K and k are constants which depend on the size and shape of the object.

Exercise 1

1. The examples in the picture show (i) a sky-diver free-falling, (ii) a person using a parachute, (iii) a rhinoceros using an identical parachute.

    If the resistance force in each example is of the form $R = kv^2$, for which situation would k be (a) smallest, (b) largest?

    (i)   (ii)   (iii)

2. The resistance force on a wooden block when in orientation A is $R = 16v$ newtons. What would be the resistance force on the block falling in orientation B?

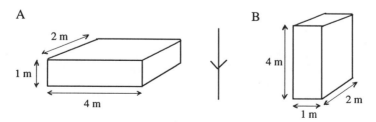

3. Two identical cones are dropped from a high tower, one base first and one point first. The cross-sectional areas of the cones are equal. Comment on the size of the resistance force on each cone.

1.3   Modelling a sky-diver's descent

Imagine a sky-diver making a jump from 3700 metres. At first, she accelerates at approximately 10 ms^{-2} since the air resistance is small. At this rate, after 5 seconds she would be travelling at 50 ms^{-1} and would continue to accelerate. However, this does not happen because the air resistance quickly becomes significant. The resistance force or drag gradually increases as her speed increases. At some point, the resistance force balances her weight of 600 newtons and she stops accelerating. From then on she will travel with constant speed, her terminal speed.

At terminal speed, the weight is balanced by the air resistance force,

i.e. $mg = R$

Hence there is no resultant force and so the acceleration is zero.

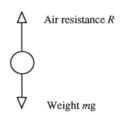

Air resistance R

Weight mg

> **For a body falling from rest through air, the resistance increases with speed until it balances the weight. The body then falls with constant terminal speed because there is no acceleration.**

(a)   Model the sky-diver with a force diagram.

(b)   Assume that her terminal speed is 50 ms^{-1} and that air resistance is modelled by the force $R = Kv$. Hence deduce the value of K.

(c)   Show how Newton's second law can be used to obtain the differential equation of motion:

$$\frac{dv}{dt} = 10 - 0.2v$$

The graph shows the direction field produced by a solution sketcher for solutions to the equation $\frac{dv}{dt} = 10 - 0.2v$.

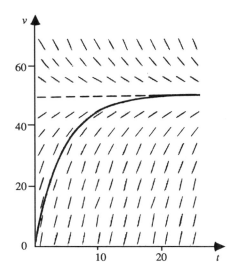

By starting the numerical solution at (0, 0), you can obtain a solution for $v(t)$ which is relevant to the sky-diver jumping with zero initial speed. You can check that it takes about 20 seconds for her to 'more or less' reach terminal speed.

By starting from other points, you can obtain solutions relevant to other situations.

> **Sketch and interpret solutions which pass through the points:**
>
> (a)   **(5, 0)**
> (b)   **(0, 10)**
> (c)   **(0, 50)**
> (d)   **(0, 60)**
>
> **Think of some real situations which would have these initial conditions.**

You can also obtain numerical solutions by using the Euler step method. The sky-diver's descent will be analysed again in Tasksheet 2, using a program to obtain a numerical solution. An alternative model for the air resistance force, $R = kv^2$, will be used for comparison.

TASKSHEET 2 – *Free-fall*

5

Example 1

A large ball is thrown vertically upwards with a speed of 8 ms⁻¹. It has a mass of 100 grams. The resistance force due to the air, R newtons, is modelled by $R = 0.25v$, where v ms⁻¹ is the speed of the ball.

Using a numerical method find the maximum height the ball reaches above the point of projection.

Solution

```
Set up a model
```

Assume that the only forces acting on the ball are its weight and air resistance. Let h metres be the height of the centre of mass of the ball above the ground. Initially, $h = 0$. Assume g $= 10$ ms⁻².

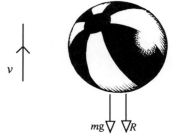

```
Analyse the problem
```

Using Newton's second law upwards:

$$0.1 \frac{dv}{dt} = -0.1g - 0.25v \implies \frac{dv}{dt} = -10 - 2.5v$$

Using the Euler step method program with a step size of 0.01 second, the expression for the acceleration is $a = -10 - 2.5v$.

The table shows results for the first 4 steps, and is then continued until $v \le 0$ (i.e. until the maximum height has been reached).

Time $t_{n+1} = t_n + 0.01$	Speed $v_{n+1} = v_n + 0.01a_n$	Acceleration $a_{n+1} = -10 - 2.5v_n$	Height $h_{n+1} = h_n + 0.01v_n$
0.00	8.0	− 30.0	0.00
0.01	7.7	− 30.0	0.08
0.02	7.4	− 29.3	0.16
0.03	7.1	− 28.5	0.23
0.04	6.8	− 27.8	0.30
....	continue until $v \le 0$		....
0.41	0.1	− 10.6	1.43
0.42	0.0	− 10.3	1.43
0.43	− 0.1	− 10.1	1.43

When $v \approx 0$, the ball has reached 1.43 metres. To obtain a more accurate answer for the maximum height, i.e. when the speed is exactly zero, a smaller step size should be used, for example, 0.005 or 0.001. Decreasing the step size will give a more accurate solution providing the step size is not so small that rounding errors are compounded.

> **Numerical methods can be used to solve any differential equation. The step size should be as small as is practical. A very small step size may be too time-consuming.**

Exercise 2

(In the following questions take $g = 10$ ms^{-2}.)

1.   A mouse of mass 45 grams falls from the top of a building 12 metres high. Air resistance is modelled by the force $R = 0.3v$ newtons, where v ms^{-1} is the speed of the mouse.

   (a)   Show that the differential equation for the fall is:

$$\frac{dv}{dt} = 10 - \frac{20v}{3}$$

   (b)   Use the step-by-step method to calculate the time taken for the mouse to fall 12 metres. (A suggested step size is 0.01 second.)

   (c)   Find the speed of the mouse on impact.

   (d)   Repeat the calculations with step sizes of 0.005 and 0.001. Compare the results for the time of fall.

2.   A water-skier is pulled from rest by a speed-boat exerting a constant horizontal force of 180 newtons. The mass of the skier and her skis is 60 kg. Her maximum speed is 9 ms^{-1}. The total resistance force due to the water and air is modelled by $R = Kv$ newtons, where v ms^{-1} is her speed.

   (a)   Draw a force diagram for the water-skier when moving at 9 ms^{-1}.

   (b)   Calculate the value of the constant K.

   (c)   Write down the equation of motion for the skier.

3. The motion of a downhill skier, of mass 65 kg, is modelled by the equation of motion:

$$65 \, g \sin 20 - 0.5v^2 = 65\frac{dv}{dt}$$

(a) State three main assumptions that have been made to obtain the equation of motion.

(b) Calculate the terminal speed of the skier.

4. The skier in question 3 assumes a more tucked position so the resistance force is now modelled as $R = 0.2v^2$.

(a) Calculate her new terminal speed.

(b) Use a step-by-step method to find her time to complete a course 2.5 km long.

1.4 Terminal speed

For most of free-fall, the sky-diver of Section 1.3 is travelling at her terminal speed. In this section you will examine this part of the motion in greater detail.

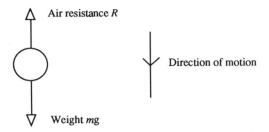

Using Newton's second law downwards:

$$mg - R = m\,\frac{dv}{dt}$$

When the resultant force acting on a moving object is zero, it will continue to move with constant velocity. It is then said to be in **dynamic equilibrium**.

So at terminal speed there is no resultant force, i.e. $mg = R$, and the acceleration is zero.

> **Two models for the resistance force have been suggested:**
> $$R = Kv \text{ and } R = kv^2$$
>
> **Given a terminal speed of w metres per second, show that these models lead respectively to the following expressions for w:**
> $$w = \frac{mg}{K} \text{ and } w = \sqrt{\left(\frac{mg}{k}\right)}$$

The graphs for both resistance models show how the terminal speed, w, of an object varies as its mass increases (with no change in the size or shape of the object).

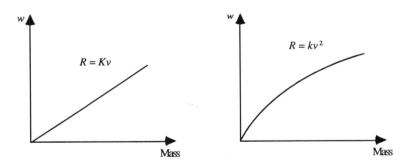

(a) Interpret the expressions $w = \frac{mg}{K}$ and $w = \sqrt{\left(\frac{mg}{k}\right)}$.

(b) Explain how a sky-diver is able to change terminal speed during the free-fall.

(c) Why is the sky-diver's terminal speed much slower once the parachute is opened?

(d) Would the sky-diver have the same terminal speed on the Moon?

(e) Explain why, when two or more sky-divers link up in free-fall, their terminal speed does not increase significantly .

It is possible to use a simple experiment to investigate how terminal speed varies with mass. The data can be used to validate one of the models for the resistance force. If terminal speed is proportional to mass, then the $R = Kv$ model is appropriate. However, if terminal speed is proportional to the square root of mass, then $R = kv^2$ is a better model.

TASKSHEET 3 – *Resistance experiments*

In experiments where the speeds are low, $R = Kv$ is an appropriate model for the air resistance force. However, when the speeds are higher, $R = kv^2$ is a more suitable model.

In addition, it can be found from experiment that the resistance force is proportional to the cross-sectional area of the object.

Exercise 3

1. In a wind tunnel experiment, a small disc is placed in the air flow. A balance is used to measure the resistance force, R newtons, for different wind speeds. The data collected are recorded below.

Wind speed (ms⁻¹)	7.46	10.06	15.09	19.22	21.21	24.53
Resistance force (N)	0.27	0.49	1.11	1.78	2.18	3.03

Find a suitable function to model the resistance force in terms of the wind speed.

2. In an experiment, spheres of different masses, but equal diameter, were dropped in a long column of oil. The time taken to travel a distance of one metre was found, after each sphere had reached terminal speed.

Mass (grams)	8.25	2.66	2.31	1.225
Terminal speed (ms^{-1})	0.704	0.235	0.188	0.040

(a) Plot the data on suitable axes.

(b) What type of model for the resistance force seems most appropriate, $R = Kv$ or $R = kv^2$?

(c) Calculate the value of K or k.

3. An A4 sheet of card falling vertically through the air is found to have a terminal speed of w ms^{-1}. At such slow speeds, $R = Kv$ was found to be a good model of the air resistance, where K is proportional to the surface area of the card.

w ms^{-1}

Predict the terminal speeds, in terms of w, for the following objects:

(a) two pieces of A4 card stuck face to face;

(b) an A3 (double sized) sheet of the card;

(c) half of an A4 sheet of card;

(d) an A4 sheet folded in half.

1.5 Another force – upthrust

Consider the motion of an airship rising slowly after its mooring ropes are released. What forces are acting on it and how should they be modelled?

It is clear that there is a resultant force acting on the airship.

The force due to air resistance, R, and the weight, W, of the airship act down and there is a force U acting upwards called the **upthrust**.

Until now the effects of upthrust have been ignored in the setting up of a model. However, any body totally or partially immersed in a fluid, such as air, water, oil, etc., experiences an upwards force due to the pressure of the surrounding fluid.

The effect of upthrust can be demonstrated by lowering an object on a newton meter into water. The decrease in the reading on the meter is the magnitude of the upthrust force of the water on the object.

The model for upthrust is based on Archimedes' principle:

$$\text{Upthrust} = \text{Weight of fluid displaced}$$

Alternatively, $U = \rho V g$

where ρ kg m^{-3} is the density of displaced fluid, V m^3 is the volume of the body, and g ms^{-2} is the acceleration due to gravity.

> **(a)** Describe how the upthrust on the airship might vary as it rises to the stratosphere.
>
> **(b)** Why is the upthrust due to air negligible for a cannon-ball, but significant for a child's helium balloon?

The equation of motion of the airship would be:

$$U - W - R = m \frac{dv}{dt}$$

where m kilograms is the mass of the fully inflated airship.

Exercise 4

(In the following questions take g $=$ 10 ms^{-2}.)

1. Two metal spheres of equal radius 10 cm, one of lead (density 11000 kg m^{-3}) and the other of iron (density 8000 kg m^{-3}) are dropped into a tank of water. The resistance force on each sphere due to the water is modelled as $R = 16v$ newtons where v ms^{-1} is the speed of the sphere.

   (a) Derive an equation of motion for each sphere if upthrust is not ignored.

   (b) Calculate their terminal speeds.

2. Estimate the upthrust force on yourself:

   (a) in air of density 1.29 kg m^{-3},

   (b) floating in water,

   (c) fully immersed in water.

3. A balloon has a volume of 2200 m^3 and is filled with hot air of density 0.98 kg m^{-3}. The deflated balloon, equipment and passengers together have a mass of 0.6 tonnes.

   (a) Calculate the upthrust force on the inflated balloon given that the surrounding air has density 1.29 kg m^{-3}.

   (b) Find the initial acceleration of the balloon.

   (c) What effect will air resistance have on the balloon's ascent?

After working through this chapter you should:

1.   be able to model the motion in one dimension of bodies subject to weight, upthrust and a variable resistance force (for example, air resistance);

2.   understand what is meant by the terms terminal speed and dynamic equilibrium;

3.   know that accepted models for resistance are:

Kv for low speed

and kv^2 for high speed;

4.   be able to solve, by the step-by-step method, first order differential equations of the form:

$$\frac{dv}{dt} = f(v)$$

5.   be able to interpret graphical and numerical solutions to problems in the context of resisted motion.

Sky-diving

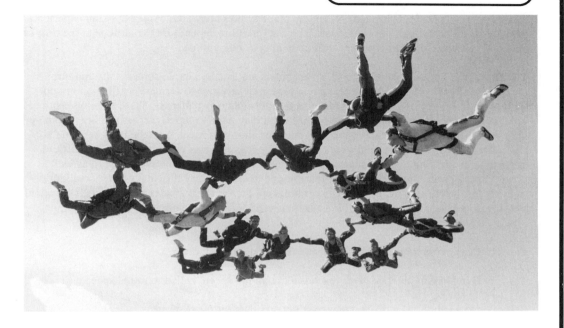

Read the following article carefully.

As the sky-diver stands at the door of the aeroplane nearly 12 000 ft. (3700 m) up, the Earth below is a patchwork of colour seen through patches of cloud, with houses almost too small to be picked out. The aeroplane arrives at the jump point and the sky-diver launches herself into space – arms and legs outstretched, body arched slightly backwards, head pulled up. Her speed increases for about eight seconds, reaching a 'terminal speed' of approximately 120 m.p.h. (190 km h^{-1}). This is the highest speed she will achieve in this position. Her altimeter tells her the height, second by second, as she plunges earthward and she knows that to make a safe land-ing, she must open her parachute before she reaches 2000 ft. (610 m). So the free-fall will last less than one minute – a brief, floating interlude during which the parachutist carries out the acrobatics which are the real purpose of sky-diving. As she completes the sky-dive she opens her parachute and directs her approach to the landing spot by controlling the two steering lines.

Sky-divers use many different types of parachute, but the principles are much the same. The type of parachute used by beginners is the familiar circular canopy with two L-shaped gaps cut at the back. As air rushes through these gaps, it produces a forward thrust which enables the para-chutist to steer to the landing place, otherwise she would drift with the wind. In still air, she travels forward at what, on land, would be a brisk walking speed. Whatever type of canopy is used – round or square – the jumper is suspended in a nylon harness. Four nylon strips called 'risers' connect the harness to the rigging lines of the canopy. Two steering lines from the canopy allow the jumper to steer left or right by pulling on them. The jumper also has an emer-gency parachute, in case the first should malfunction. Sky-divers always pack their own para-chutes, initially under careful supervision.

(continued)

For most jumps, a small, high-winged aircraft, such as the three-passenger Cessna 172, is used. If several sky-divers are jumping together, a larger aircraft, such as a Short's Sky Van, which carries up to 16 people, is needed. When the plane arrives above the chosen spot, an experienced parachutist dives through the open door. The free-fall time depends on the altitude at the time of exit, and can be as short as eight seconds or as long as one minute.

The first aerial gymnastics performed by beginners are usually simple somersaults and turns in the air. As sky-divers become more experienced, they advance to formation falls, joining up with other sky-divers to complete a series of rapidly changing patterns. These displays require great skill, as the divers are travelling at speed and may have to 'track' across the sky to join up with the other divers. To achieve this they must be almost vertical, with the body forming a slight curve. Arms must be held to the side and the legs together and extended. The 'lift' created by air passing over her curved body causes the parachutist to travel forward as well as down. The forward movement can be fast enough to cause injury if two sky-divers collide. So to break the speed, a parachutist brings her arms up, presenting a greater area to the air flow and slowing down her body. This skill must be mastered before she can join in formation jumps.

1.   Draw a diagram showing the forces acting on the sky-diver.

2.   Explain why the sky-diver reaches a maximum speed, called terminal speed.

3.   How can the sky-diver increase or decrease her terminal speed?

4.   From the text or your own experience, describe how the air resistance force is related to speed.

5.   Sketch a possible graph of resistance against speed and suggest a suitable function for this relationship.

Free-fall

A sky-diver jumps from a plane at a height of 3700 metres. In order to make a safe landing, the parachute must be opened before a height of 610 metres is reached.

Problem   To estimate the length of time the sky-diver is in free-fall.

Set up a model

Let the air resistance be modelled by the force $R = kv^2$ newtons.

1.   List the other assumptions about mass, motion and terminal speed for the sky-diver which were made in Section 1.3. Hence obtain the equation of motion:

$$\frac{dv}{dt} = 10 - 0.004v^2$$

Analyse the problem

An Euler step method can be used to calculate the velocity, acceleration and height of the sky-diver after successive small increments of time.

From the equation of motion above, the acceleration $a = 10 - 0.004v^2$.
The speed is found by considering a small change in time of dt.

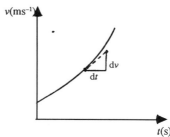

Then the acceleration is $a = \frac{dv}{dt}$

$$\Rightarrow dv = a \, dt.$$

From the graph, the new speed is approximately

$$v_1 = v_0 + dv = v_0 + a \, dt$$

Similarly, the change in height is approximately $dh = v_0 \, dt$.

Since the sky-diver is falling, the new height $h_1 = h_0 - dh \Rightarrow h_1 = h_0 - v_0 \, dt$.

The table shows the first few calculations in the process for a step size dt of 0.1 second.

Time $t_{n+1} = t_n + 0.1$	Velocity $v_{n+1} = v_n + 0.1a_n$	Acceleration $a_{n+1} = 10 - 0.004v_n{}^2$	Height $h_{n+1} = h_n - 0.1v_n$
0	0	10	3700
0.1	1.00	10.000	3700.0
0.2	2.00	9.996	3699.9
0.3	3.00	9.984	3699.7
0.4	4.00	9.964	3699.4
...	...	...	...

Many steps are required for a complete solution. To save time, it is possible to write a short program for a computer or a calculator to perform these calculations. (See the programs at the end of this book.)

2.   Use a program to check the calculations in the table in question 1 and complete the calculations for the first second of the motion.
(Save your program as you will use it again in this unit.)

3.   By adapting your program, calculate the velocity and height at regular intervals (for example, every 1 or 5 seconds) and use the results to plot the graphs of speed V and height H against time for the descent to 610 metres.

4.   How long does it take the sky-diver to approximately reach her terminal speed?

5.   How long can she spend in free-fall?

Interpret/validate

The article in Tasksheet 1 stated:

'Her speed increases for about eight seconds, reaching a 'terminal speed' of approximately 120 m.p.h.(190 km h^{-1}). This is the highest speed she will achieve in this position. Her altimeter tells her the height, second by second, as she plunges earthward, and she knows that to make a safe landing, she must open her parachute before she reaches 2000 ft. (610 m). So the free-fall will last less than one minute – a brief, floating interlude during which the parachutist carries out the acrobatics which are the real purpose of sky-diving.'

6.   Use the information above to validate your solution. Try to account for any discrepancies.

7E.   Investigate the accuracy of your solution by changing the step size.

Resistance experiments

 Problem To find an appropriate model for the resistance force in a practical situation.

1.   Choose or design a simple experiment for which the resistance force is significant.

Some suggestions, shown in the picture, are:

   •   a falling ball with a sail;

   •   weights sinking in a long tube filled with water;

   •   a balloon (possibly filled with helium) with light weights (such as paper clips) attached;

   •   a parachute made from polystyrene, card or a carrier bag;

   •   a set of paper bun cases that can be stacked together to increase mass.

2.   Collect data for the time taken to travel a range of distances.

3.   Plot the graph of distance against time and use it to estimate the terminal speed of the object.

4.   Vary the mass of the object, taking care not to alter its shape or size significantly, and find its new terminal speed.

5.   Collect data to sketch a graph and find a relationship between terminal speed and mass.

6.   Suggest an appropriate model for the resistance force.

Tutorial sheet

1. The graph shows the direction field for the equation of motion of a parachutist falling at $v \text{ ms}^{-1}$,

$$\frac{dv}{dt} = 5 - v$$

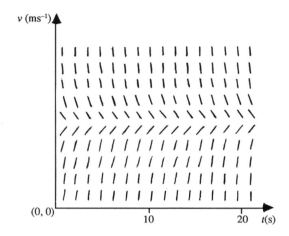

(a) Sketch the solution for which the parachutist is falling with constant speed. Hence indicate the scale on the v-axis on the above graph.

(b) Sketch the solution for which the parachutist is initially at rest.

(c) If the parachutist were to fall from rest, use the graph or a solution sketcher to determine how long would it take for him to reach 4.5 ms^{-1}.

2. A sky-diver of mass 80 kg is travelling at terminal speed, 50 ms^{-1}, in her free-fall position.

(a) Draw a diagram showing the magnitude and direction of the forces acting on the sky-diver.

(b) Estimate the new resistance force if the sky-diver quickly curls herself up into a tight ball, presenting about half her original cross-sectional area to the oncoming air.

(c) Calculate her acceleration just after she curls herself up.

(continued)

3. For the models of air resistance, $R = Kv$ or $R = kv^2$, the velocity v is actually the **relative** velocity of the object through the medium.

    The equation of motion of a car of mass m kilograms moving at speed v ms⁻¹ in still air is modelled by

    $$T - Kv = m\, \frac{dv}{dt}$$

    where T and K are constants.

    (a) Deduce the equation of motion for the same car moving against a headwind of 10 ms⁻¹.

    (b) What effect does the headwind have on the car's maximum speed?

    (c) Explain the slipstreaming effect which allows a racing car to make use of the slipstream behind another vehicle.

4. A man of mass 70 kg is skiing in a straight line down a slope of gradient $\tan \theta$. The resistance force is modelled by $R = kv^2$ newtons where v ms⁻¹ is the skier's speed.

    (a) Derive an equation of motion for the skier.

    (b) Express the maximum speed of the skier, V, in terms of k and θ.

    (c) What happens to the maximum speed as θ varies?

2   *Analytical methods*

2.1   Motion at 'low' speeds

In this section, you will solve the differential equation for resisted motion at low speeds using the method of separation of variables. This will give an algebraic solution which is more powerful than numerical solutions such as those obtained in Chapter 1. (The method of integration by separation of variables is an example of an 'analytical method'.)

Consider the motion of a weighted bob tied on the end of a thin cord and being used to test the depth of water in a river.

Problem To find a general solution for the motion of the bob as it sinks to the bottom.

Set up a model

The following assumptions are made.

- The bob is a particle of mass m kilograms.
- The cord is light and does not restrict the motion of the bob in any way.
- The force due to upthrust on the bob is negligible.
- The bob enters the water with zero speed.
- The model used for the resistance force at low speed is $R = Kv$ newtons, where K is a constant and the speed of the bob is v ms^{-1}.

Hence the only forces acting on the bob are its weight and water resistance.

Analyse the problem

Newton's second law:

$$mg - R = m\,\frac{dv}{dt}$$

Substituting $R = Kv$:

$$mg - Kv = m\,\frac{dv}{dt} \implies \frac{dv}{dt} = g - \frac{Kv}{m}$$

Separating variables:

$$\int \frac{dv}{\left(g - \frac{Kv}{m}\right)} = \int dt$$

$$-\frac{m}{K}\ln\left| g - \frac{Kv}{m} \right| = t + \text{constant}$$

The initial conditions are $t = 0$ and $v = 0$.

$$\Rightarrow \quad \text{constant} = -\frac{m}{K} \ln |g|$$

and so $\quad t = -\frac{m}{K} \ln \left| g - \frac{Kv}{m} \right| + \frac{m}{K} \ln |g|$

Rearranging for v:

$$\frac{-Kt}{m} = \ln \left| \frac{g - \frac{Kv}{m}}{g} \right| \quad \Rightarrow \quad e^{-\frac{Kt}{m}} = 1 - \frac{Kv}{mg}$$

Therefore the speed of the falling bob at time t is:

$$v = \frac{mg}{K} \left(1 - e^{-\frac{Kt}{m}} \right)$$

Interpret/validate

This is a general solution which applies to any object falling under gravity, where the resistance force is modelled by $R = Kv$. Using this expression with appropriate values for the constants, graphs can easily be sketched to compare the motion of bodies of different mass, size and shape. The graphs show speed against time for identically-shaped bobs of different masses, where $K = 5$.

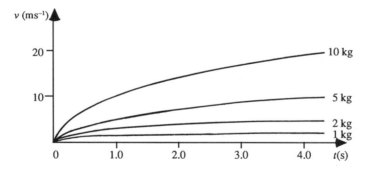

(a) **Interpret these graphs, referring to the acceleration and terminal speed of the bob.**

(b) **By integrating the expression for v, show that the distance fallen, x, is given by:**

$$x = \frac{mg}{K} \left(t + \frac{m}{K} \left(e^{-\frac{Kt}{m}} - 1 \right) \right)$$

(c) **Draw graphs of distance against time for identically-shaped bobs of masses 1, 2, 5 and 10 kg, where $K = 5$.**

TASKSHEET 1 – *A falling feather*

Solutions obtained numerically can now be checked with this general solution. For instance, graphs from the general solution can be superimposed on the numerical solutions.

The advantage of a general solution is that it enables much more interpretation, for example, of the effects of changing parameters such as mass. It is easier to sketch graphs for different values of the parameters K and m, instead of solving the equation numerically each time. Even for a particular case, it may be quicker, more accurate and more reliable to substitute particular values into your general solutions.

Acceleration can be written in various forms:

$$\frac{dv}{dt} = v\frac{dv}{dx} = \frac{d^2x}{dt^2}$$

The choice depends on the final solution required.

For solutions in v and t, use $\dfrac{dv}{dt}$.

For solutions in v and x, use $v\dfrac{dv}{dx}$.

For solutions in x and t, use $\dfrac{d^2x}{dt^2}$.

Example 1

A fisherman casts a line with a spinner attached to the end. The spinner sinks slowly in the water before being reeled in, imitating the movement of a small fish.

The fisherman chooses a spinner of mass 30 grams, which sinks with terminal speed $1.5\ \text{ms}^{-1}$.

(a) Find a suitable model for the force due to the water resistance.

(b) Calculate the depth to which the spinner sinks in 3 seconds.

(c) Estimate the time taken for the spinner to fall to a depth of 15 metres.

Solution

Assume that the spinner is small in comparison with its weight. The upthrust force is then negligible. Assume the spinner sinks vertically downwards, entering the water at time $t = 0$ with speed $v = 0$. For low speeds, the appropriate model for resistance is $R = Kv$ newtons. Let x metres be the depth to which the spinner sinks in time t seconds. Take $g = 10\ \text{ms}^{-2}$.

Thus the only forces acting on the spinner are its weight and water resistance.

(a) Newton's second law:

$$0.3 - Kv = 0.03 \frac{dv}{dt}$$

At terminal speed, $K \times 1.5 = 0.3 \Rightarrow K = 0.2$

Hence a suitable model for the force due to the water resistance is $R = 0.2v$.

(b) Substituting $K = 0.2$ in the equation of motion:

$$\frac{dv}{dt} = \frac{10}{3}(3 - 2v)$$

Separating variables and integrating:

$$\int_0^v \frac{1}{3-2v}\, dv = \int_0^t \frac{10}{3}\, dt \Rightarrow -\frac{1}{2}\ln|\,3 - 2v\,| + \frac{1}{2}\ln 3 = \frac{10t}{3}$$

Rearranging this:

$$\ln\left|\frac{3-2v}{3}\right| = \frac{-20}{3}t \Rightarrow v = 1.5\left(1 - e^{-\frac{20}{3}t}\right)$$

Integrating again for depth x at time t:

$$\int_0^x dx = \int_0^t 1.5\left(1 - e^{-\frac{20}{3}t}\right)dt = \left[1.5\left(t + \frac{3}{20}e^{-\frac{20}{3}t}\right)\right]_0^t$$

$$\Rightarrow x = 1.5\left(t + \frac{3}{20}\left(e^{-\frac{20}{3}t} - 1\right)\right)$$

Substituting $t = 3$ into this expression gives $x = 4.275$ metres. In 3 seconds, the spinner will have sunk to a depth of 4.3 metres.

(c) Substituting $t = 3$ into the expression for $v(t)$, after 3 seconds the spinner is almost travelling at its terminal speed of 1.5 ms⁻¹.

Assume that for the remaining distance of 10.725 metres the spinner is travelling at 1.5 ms⁻¹,

$$\Rightarrow t = 3 + \frac{10.725}{1.5} = 10.15$$

The time taken to sink 15 metres is 10.15 seconds. This gives an average speed of 1.48 ms⁻¹, almost the terminal speed of the spinner.

Note that, for large enough t, you can use the approximation

$$x \approx 1.5\left(t - \frac{3}{20}\right).$$

Exercise 1   (In the following questions take g = 10 ms⁻².)

1.   A child lets go of a helium-filled balloon of mass 0.02 kg and it slowly rises. The equation of motion for the balloon is given by:

$$1 - 0.5v = 0.02 \frac{dv}{dt}$$

where v ms⁻¹ is the speed of the balloon.

(a)   State the forces acting on the balloon in this model and draw a force diagram. Find the magnitude of the upthrust force.

(b)   Calculate the terminal speed of the balloon.

2.   A tug boat is towing a ferry of mass 6000 tonnes by means of a single horizontal cable. The ferry experiences a resistance to motion given by $R = 12\,000v$ newtons, where v ms⁻¹ is the speed of the ferry.

(a)   Draw a diagram of the forces acting on the ferry.

(b)   Find the tension in the cable when the ferry is pulled at a steady speed of 1.5 ms⁻¹.

3.   A small chick of mass 110 grams falls from a branch 12 metres above the ground. The chick's descent is slowed by air resistance, upthrust due to the air and the flapping of the chick's wings. The air resistance force is modelled by $R = 0.7v$ newtons where v ms⁻¹ is the speed of the chick and the upthrust force is 0.12 newtons.

(a)   Write down an equation of motion for the chick's descent.

(b)   Find the chick's terminal speed.

(c)   By integrating twice, find an expression for the distance fallen in terms of time.

(d)   Draw a graph of distance against time for the fall and hence find the time taken for the fall.

4.   A feather and a marble are dropped at the same time from a 30 metre high tower on a calm still day. The marble can be modelled as a particle of mass 0.5 kg for which air resistance is negligible. The feather is of mass 0.006 kg and the air resistance force is modelled as $R = 0.05v$ newtons where v ms⁻¹ is the speed of the feather.

(a)   Find an expression for the velocity of the feather after time t seconds. Hence deduce the terminal speed of the feather.

(b)   Find the time taken for the feather to reach 99% of its terminal speed.

(c)   Calculate the times taken for the marble and the feather to reach the ground.

(d)   What are the speeds of the marble and the feather on impact?

2.2   Motion at 'high' speed

In this section you will return to the problem of the sky-diver. A sky-diver in free-fall is one example of motion at high speed, so the air resistance force is modelled by $R = kv^2$. You have already obtained a numerical solution to the equation of motion for a sky-diver using this model for air resistance. You will now obtain a general solution.

 Problem   To find how the speed varies with time for the motion of a sky-diver.

Set up a model

The following assumptions are made.

- The sky-diver is a particle of mass m kilograms.
- She is in free-fall, with no cross-winds, and falls from rest.
- The model used for the resistance force at high speed is $R = kv^2$, where k is constant and v ms^{-1} is the speed of the sky-diver.
- Let w ms^{-1} be the terminal speed of the sky-diver.

Analyse the problem

Newton's second law:

$$mg - kv^2 = m\,\frac{dv}{dt}$$

At terminal speed:

$$mg = kw^2 \;\Rightarrow\; k = \frac{mg}{w^2}$$

$$\Rightarrow\; mg - \frac{mg}{w^2}\,v^2 = m\,\frac{dv}{dt}$$

$$\Rightarrow\; \frac{dv}{dt} = -\frac{g}{w^2}\,(v^2 - w^2)$$

$$\Rightarrow\; \int_0^v \frac{1}{v^2 - w^2}\,dv = \int_0^t \frac{-g}{w^2}\,dt$$

(a)   **Show that** $\dfrac{1}{2w}\,\ln\left|\dfrac{w - v}{w + v}\right| = -\dfrac{gt}{w^2}$

(b)   **Hence show that** $v = w\left(\dfrac{1 - e^{-\frac{2gt}{w}}}{1 + e^{-\frac{2gt}{w}}}\right)$

This is a general solution for any object falling from rest under gravity, where the resistance force is modelled by $R = kv^2$.

> **Sketch the graph of speed against time for the sky-diver where $w = 50$ and $g = 10$.**
>
> **Verify that $v \to w$ as $t \to +\infty$.**

To continue with this analysis to find an expression for the distance fallen at time t would require integration of the expression above. Although this is possible, it is a difficult integration. This is one of the disadvantages of analytical methods.

	Advantages	Disadvantages
Analytical method:	Algebraic solutions are general and give exact answers. They facilitate interpretation.	It may be difficult or even impossible to find a solution.
Numerical method:	A numerical solution is always possible.	Only particular cases can be solved. Solutions are subject to inaccuracies.

 TASKSHEET 2 – *Opening the parachute*

Example 2

A tennis ball of mass 0.1 kg is projected vertically upwards from a height of 1 metre with an initial speed of 12 ms^{-1}. The air resistance force is modelled as $R = 0.0025v^2$ newtons, where v ms^{-1} is the speed of the ball. Find the time taken for the ball to reach its maximum height, i.e. the height at which $v = 0$.

Solution

Newton's second law upwards:

$$-1 - 0.0025v^2 = 0.1\frac{dv}{dt}$$

$$\Rightarrow \quad -(400 + v^2) = 40\frac{dv}{dt}$$

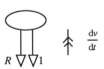

Separating variables and integrating:

$$\int_0^t -\frac{1}{40}\,dt = \int_{12}^0 \frac{1}{400 + v^2}\,dv$$

$$\Rightarrow \quad -\frac{t}{40} = 0 - \frac{1}{20}\tan^{-1}\left(\frac{12}{20}\right) \Rightarrow t = 2\tan^{-1}(0.6) = 1.08$$

The time taken for the ball to reach its maximum height is 1.08 seconds.

Exercise 2   (In the following questions take g = 10 ms^{-2}.)

1.   For the tennis ball in Example 2:

   (a)   calculate the maximum height above the ground that the ball reaches;

   (b)   compare this with the maximum height it would reach if the resistance were zero.

2.   A speed boat of mass 1200 kg is travelling at 30 ms^{-1} in calm water when the engine cuts out. When moving at v ms^{-1}, the force due to water resistance on the boat is λv^2 newtons where λ is a constant.

   (a)   Write down a differential equation of motion for the boat.

   (b)   Show that the speed v at time t seconds after the engine cuts out is:

$$v = \frac{1200}{\lambda t + 40}$$

   (c)   It is observed that the speed slows down to 10 ms^{-1} in 5 seconds. Use this information to find the value of λ. Hence find how long it takes for the speed to slow to 5 ms^{-1}.

3.   A ski-jumper of mass 80 kg slides from rest down the smooth take-off ramp, inclined at 30° to the horizontal. The ramp is 85 metres long. The air resistance R newtons acting on the ski-jumper when on the ramp is modelled by $R = 0.64\ v^2$, where v ms^{-1} is the speed of the ski-jumper.

   (a)   Find the speed of the ski-jumper at the end of the ramp.

   (b)   Comment on the change in the air resistance force when the jumper leaves the ramp.

4.   A car of mass 1.8 tonnes is initially travelling at 28 ms^{-1}. The engine is turned off and the car free-wheels to rest.

   The horizontal force acting on the free-wheeling car has two components:

   •   a constant force of 144 newtons due to friction;
   •   a resistance of $36v^2$ newtons, where v ms^{-1} is the speed of the car.

   (a)   Show that the differential equation of motion for the car is:

$$\frac{dv}{dt} = \frac{-(4 + v^2)}{50}$$

   (b)   Find the time taken for the car to free-wheel to rest.

2.3   Modelling resisted motion

There are many situations that can be investigated using the ideas in this chapter. You may have noticed some of them as you worked through the examples.

> **All the situations in the picture above could be modelled using the differential equations in this chapter. What problems does the picture suggest that you could investigate? What assumptions should you make in each case?**

After working through this chapter you should:

1. be able to solve by analytical methods first order differential equations of the form:

$$v \frac{dv}{dx} = f(v) \text{ or } \frac{dv}{dt} = f(v)$$

2. be aware of a variety of situations which can be modelled using these differential equations;

3. be able to interpret graphical, algebraic and numerical solutions to problems in the context of resisted motion;

4. know the advantages and disadvantages of numerical and analytical methods.

A falling feather

Feathers of all kinds fall slowly because their motion is greatly dependent on air resistance. For such a feather of mass m kilograms, assume that the air resistance force is modelled by $R = Kv$ newtons and assume a terminal speed of w ms^{-1}.

1. Express K in terms of m and w.

2. Show that the equation of motion for the feather travelling at speed v ms^{-1} can be written as:

$$\frac{dv}{dt} = g\left(1 - \frac{v}{w}\right)$$

3. Interpret this expression for the acceleration when:

    (a) $v < w$; (b) $v = w$; (c) $v > w$.

4. Integrate the expression and show that, for a feather falling from rest, the solution for v is:

$$v = w\left(1 - e^{-\frac{gt}{w}}\right)$$

5. Does the feather actually reach terminal speed? Comment on your answer.

6. Taking $w = 1$, use a graphical method or otherwise to find the time taken for the feather to reach the following percentages of terminal speed:

    (a) 50%; (b) 90%; (c) 99%.

7. Interpret these results and comment on their validity for a falling feather.

Instead of finding an expression for speed in terms of time, there are situations in which the speed at different heights is required and so a function $v(x)$ is more appropriate.

8. (a) Show that an alternative form for the acceleration $\frac{dv}{dt}$ is $v\frac{dv}{dx}$.

    (b) Using this form of acceleration, rewrite the equation of motion for the feather.

9. Show that $\frac{v}{v-w} = 1 + \frac{w}{v-w}$ and hence show that the equation of motion has a solution

$$x = \frac{-w}{g}\left(v + w \ln\left|\frac{v-w}{w}\right|\right)$$

10. Sketch the graph of distance fallen against speed. (Assume $w = 1$.)

11. Find the distance the feather has to fall to reach the following percentages of terminal speed:

    (a) 50%; (b) 90%; (c) 99%.

32

Opening the parachute

At some point, the sky-diver must end her free-fall and slow down before landing. She pulls the rip cord and releases her parachute. Her speed is high even with the parachute open, so $R = kv^2$ is still an appropriate model for the air resistance force.

 Problem
What is the least height at which the parachute can be opened in order to make a safe landing?

Set up a model

1.
   - Make some simplifying assumptions about the sky-diver's motion, including her initial speed, U, before the parachute is opened; the terminal speed, W, with the parachute; and a reasonable 'safe' landing speed, V.
   - Use $R = kv^2$ as the model for the air resistance force.
   - Let H metres be the least height at which the parachute could be opened.

2. Draw a diagram of the forces acting on the parachutist as she slows down, indicating the direction of the resultant force.

Analyse the problem

The problem is to find a value of H such that the increased air resistance force due to the parachute acts long enough to slow her down to a reasonable landing speed.

Since this is a problem involving speed and distance, a suitable equation of motion for the descent with a parachute is:

$$mg - kv^2 = mv \frac{dv}{dx}$$

3. From your assumptions, substitute appropriate values into this equation and solve it to obtain a function for the distance fallen, x metres, in terms of the speed, v ms^{-1}.

4. At what height must the parachute be opened to give a 'safe' landing speed.

Interpret/validate

In Tasksheet 1, Chapter 1, the article stated that 610 metres was the height at which the parachute should be opened.

5. Compare this height with the one you have calculated and comment on the validity of your model.

1.   A diver of mass 100 kg floats slowly from rest up to the surface of the sea under the action of an upthrust force of U newtons. The drag is modelled by a resistance force of $10v$ newtons, where v ms^{-1} is the speed of the diver.

(a)   Calculate the diver's terminal speed w in terms of U. Interpret this formula for different magnitudes of the upthrust force.

(b)   Show that $10\frac{dv}{dt} = w - v$.

(c)   By integrating this differential equation, show that the diver reaches 90% of terminal speed after approximately 23 seconds.

2.   The motion of a hot air balloon of mass m kilograms falling at speed v ms^{-1} is modelled by the equation

$$m\frac{dv}{dt} = (10m - U) - v^2$$

where U is a constant.

(a)   Suggest two assumptions underlying this model.

(b)   In a problem you are given that the balloon is initially at rest at a height of 1000 metres and asked to find the speed of impact with the ground. Rewrite the equation in a suitable form.

(c)   If $U = 12\,000$ and $m = 1500$, show that this speed of impact is 47 ms^{-1}.

3.   A ball is dropped down a well and t seconds later has fallen a distance x metres, where

$$x = 12\left[t + 1.2\left(e^{-5t/6} - 1\right)\right]$$

(a)   What is the ball's terminal speed?

(b)   An identical ball is dropped 1 second later. Find the distance between the two balls after t seconds. Interpret your formula.

4.   A high diver of mass 75 kg enters the water travelling at 15 ms^{-1}. When fully immersed his body experiences an upthrust of 900 newtons. The resistance force due to the water is modelled as $225v$ newtons where v ms^{-1} is the speed of the diver in the water.

(a)   Show that the equation of motion can be expressed as

$$v\frac{dv}{dx} = -3v - 2$$

where x metres is the depth of the diver.

(b)   Solve the equation and find the greatest depth the diver reaches. Comment on the validity of your solution.

3 *Variable mass and weight*

3.1   The Moon-lander

Suppose you are in a Moon-lander, preparing to descend to the Moon. You are 50 000 metres above the surface with the module in line for descent when the fuel runs out! You have a problem!

Problem   Should you panic? How long before you crash land? At what speed will the module crash onto the Moon?

Set up a model

The assumptions are:
- the initial velocity of the lander is 0 ms^{-1};
- there is no air resistance;
- the gravitational acceleration is 1.62 ms^{-2} and is constant for the whole motion.

> **(a)** Solve the problems using the assumptions above.
>
> **(b)** Which of the assumptions would you want to change in order to obtain more realistic solutions?

In *Modelling with force and motion* you saw that in some situations gravity should not be assumed to be constant. Over very large distances, the gravitational force of attraction changes significantly. This force was modelled by Isaac Newton when he proposed his law of gravitation.

> **Newton's law of gravitation**
>
> **If two particles of masses m_1 and m_2 kilograms are at a distance r metres apart, they will attract each other with a force of magnitude**
>
> $$F = \frac{G\,m_1 m_2}{r^2} \text{ newtons}$$
>
> **where $G = 6.67 \times 10^{-11}\ \text{Nm}^2\ \text{kg}^{-2}$ is the universal constant of gravitation.**

At height h metres above the surface, the weight W newtons of the Moon-lander is:

$$W = \frac{GMm}{(R+h)^2} = mg_h$$

where g_h is the acceleration due to gravity h metres above the surface, m kilograms is the mass of the lander, M kilograms is the mass of the Moon, and R metres is the radius of the Moon.

The acceleration due to gravity is therefore $g_h = \dfrac{GM}{(R+h)^2}$.

The graphs below show the acceleration due to gravity against height above the Moon's surface over three different ranges.

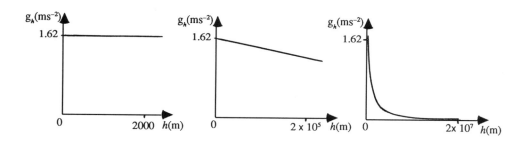

> **Interpret these graphs, suggesting which model of gravity is more appropriate for motion over the ranges shown.**

A more accurate solution to the problem at the start of this chapter can be found by using Newton's law of gravitation to model the weight of the lander.

 TASKSHEET 1 – *The Moon-lander*

> The gravitational force of a planet acting on a particle can be assumed to be constant if the motion takes place over distances which are very small compared with the radius of the planet. Otherwise Newton's law of gravitation is a more appropriate model for the gravitational force.

3.2   Escaping from the Earth

July 16th, 1969

This beast is best felt. Shake, rattle and roll! We are thrown left and right against our straps in spasmodic jerks. It is steering like crazy and I just hope it knows where it's going, because for the first ten seconds we are perilously close to the umbilical tower.

We started to burn at 100 miles altitude, and had reached only 180 miles at cut off, but we are climbing like a dingbat. In nine hours, when we are scheduled to make our first midcourse correction, we will be 57 000 miles out. At the instant of shutdown, Buzz recorded our velocity as 35 579 feet per second, more than enough to escape from the Earth's gravitational field. As we proceed outbound, this number will get smaller and smaller until the tug of the Moon's gravity exceeds that of the Earth's and then we will start speeding up again.

It's hard to believe that we are on our way to the Moon, at 1200 miles altitude now, less than three hours after lift-off, and I'll bet the launch-day crowd down at the Cape is still bumper to bumper.

Apollo expeditions to the moon (NASA)

This is Michael Collins' commentary during the launch of Apollo 11, the first manned mission to land on the Moon. The **escape speed** mentioned is the speed at which the projectile must be travelling in order to escape from the gravitational field of a planet, that is to avoid going into orbit or returning to the surface.

> **Discuss the factors involved in modelling the launch of a rocket into space.**

To simplify the problem you can eliminate some of these factors from your model and concentrate on part of the problem, namely the escape speed required. Instead of modelling a rocket, which continues to accelerate after the launch, assume that it is a projectile on which the only force acting is gravity.

Problem   Find the speed of projection, U ms^{-1}, required for a projectile to escape from a planet.

Set up a model

The assumptions are:

- air resistance is negligible;
- the attraction of other bodies is negligible;
- the projectile is a particle of mass m kilograms, and its weight varies according to Newton's law of gravitation;
- the projectile has speed v ms^{-1} and height h metres after t seconds;
- R metres is the radius, and M kilograms the mass of the planet.

Using Newton's second law and Newton's law of gravitation:

$$-\frac{GMm}{(R+h)^2} = mv\frac{dv}{dh}$$

Separating variables and integrating:

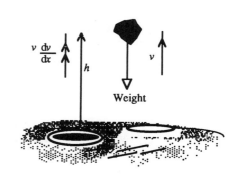

$$\int v\,dv = -\int \frac{GM}{(R+h)^2}\,dh$$

$$\Rightarrow \frac{1}{2}v^2 = \frac{GM}{(R+h)} + \text{constant}$$

The initial conditions are $h = 0$, $v = U$, giving

$$\text{constant} = \frac{1}{2}U^2 - \frac{GM}{R}$$

$$\Rightarrow v^2 = U^2 - \frac{2GMh}{R(R+h)}$$

Weight

When $v = 0$, the projectile has reached its maximum height, H.

So $U = \sqrt{\left(\frac{2GMH}{R(R+H)}\right)}$

(a) **Using a graph plotter, sketch the graph of U as a function of H for appropriate values of G, M, and R.**

(b) **Confirm that the value of the asymptote is $U = \sqrt{\left(\frac{2GM}{R}\right)}$.**

(c) **What is significant about the asymptote?**

For the projectile to escape from the planet its speed must always be greater than zero, i.e. the maximum height H is infinite.

$$U = \sqrt{\left(\frac{2GMH}{R(R+H)}\right)}$$

$$= \sqrt{\left(\frac{2GM}{R\left(\frac{R}{H}+1\right)}\right)} \to \sqrt{\left(\frac{2GM}{R}\right)} \text{ as } H \to +\infty.$$

> The escape speed of a projectile from the surface of a planet of mass M and radius R is $\sqrt{\left(\frac{2GM}{R}\right)}$.

> **Calculate the escape speed from the surface of the Earth and comment on the validity of this value.**

Example 1

A space probe discovers a small dense meteor and lands on it to take measurements. The meteor is roughly spherical, of radius 17 metres and mass 1×10^{14} kg. On leaving, the probe runs out of fuel when it is only 25 metres up, travelling directly away from the meteor at 17 ms^{-1}. Is this speed enough for the probe to escape?

Solution

Assume the probe is a particle of mass m kilograms and that there is no air resistance. Let h metres be the height of the probe above the meteor's surface and v ms^{-1} its speed.

Using Newton's second law away from the meteor:

$$-\frac{G \times 1 \times 10^{14} \times m}{(17+h)^2} = mv \frac{dv}{dh}$$

Separating variables and integrating:

$$\int_{17}^{v} v \, dv = \int_{25}^{h} -\frac{G \times 1 \times 10^{14}}{(17+h)^2} \, dh$$

$$\Rightarrow \left[\frac{v^2}{2}\right]_{17}^{v} = 6670 \left[\frac{1}{(17+h)}\right]_{25}^{h}$$

$$\Rightarrow \frac{v^2}{2} - \frac{17^2}{2} = 6670 \left(\frac{1}{17+h} - \frac{1}{42}\right)$$

If probe is to escape, then $v > 0$ as $h \to +\infty$, and so:

$$\frac{17^2}{2} + \frac{6670}{17+h} - \frac{6670}{42} > 0 \implies \frac{6670}{17+h} - 14.3 > 0$$

However, this expression is zero when $h = 449.1$. So the probe is not able to escape from the meteor and reaches a maximum height of 449 metres.

Solving the equation of motion for a projectile in a gravitational field with appropriate initial conditions gives:

$$mv \frac{dv}{dh} = -\frac{GMm}{(R+h)^2}$$

Substituting the condition $v \geq 0$ for all h, will give the escape speed.

Exercise 1

(Ignore the effects of air resistance)

1. Interpret the formula $U = \sqrt{\left(\frac{2GM}{R}\right)}$ for:

   (a) different planets;

   (b) a space station such as Skylab.

2. A tiny meteor fragment of mass 0.3 kg enters the Earth's atmosphere. At 3000 km from the surface it is travelling directly towards the Earth at a speed of 10 ms^{-1}. Calculate its speed on impact.

3. (a) Calculate the distance from the Earth where the gravitional attraction of the Earth equals that of the Moon.

   (b) Describe the motion of an unpowered craft passing through this point, travelling towards the Moon.

4. (a) In Example 1, calculate the speed of impact of the probe after it falls back to the surface of the meteor.

   (b) Calculate the minimum speed at which the probe needs to be travelling after 25 metres in order to be sure of escaping from the meteor.

5E. What is the size of the biggest asteroid that you could jump off?

[Hint: make simplifying assumptions, for example, consider the asteroid to have the same mean density as the Earth. Estimate your maximum jumping speed on Earth and calculate the mass and radius of the asteroid for which this is sufficient speed for escape.]

3.3 Rocket propulsion

Sections 3.1 and 3.2 modelled the motion of bodies which were unpowered or projected by a single initial thrust. This section will develop the model for rocket-powered motion.

A common misconception about rockets is that they are propelled by the exhaust gases actually pushing against the ground, or the air. If this were the case, how would rockets be able to travel in space? The way a rocket engine produces thrust is investigated in the tasksheet.

 TASKSHEET 2 – *Rocket propulsion*

In a jet engine, the air around the aircraft is taken in, compressed, heated by combustion with the fuel and the hot exhaust gases are ejected at high speed. A rocket engine operates by a similar principle, but, for obvious reasons it carries its own supply of oxygen to combust the fuel.

The aircraft's jet engines take air from outside, so consequently the decrease in mass is due only to the loss of fuel. The rocket, on the other hand, has a much greater change of mass because it carries both fuel and oxygen. This decrease in mass is a significant factor in modelling the motion of a rocket. The density and speed of the exhaust gas and the rate at which fuel is burnt are important in calculating the thrust produced.

 Problem   Set up a differential equation to model a rocket's motion.

The assumptions are:

- the rocket burns fuel at a constant rate, μ kilograms per second;
- the rocket is in outer space, where no external forces are acting on it;
- the exhaust gas is ejected uniformly, at a constant speed of C ms^{-1} relative to the rocket;
- the initial mass of the rocket plus fuel is M_0 kilograms.

At time t the variables are:

- the speed of the rocket, v ms^{-1};
- the mass of the rocket and remaining fuel, M kilograms;
- the mass of fuel that has been ejected, m kilograms.

Therefore $M + m = M_0$ and $\dfrac{dM}{dt} = -\dfrac{dm}{dt} = -\mu$

Consider a small interval of time, dt, during which time the mass of gas ejected is dm, resulting in an increase in speed of the rocket of dv.

Therefore $dm = \mu\, dt$ and the mass of the rocket at time t is $M(t) = M_0 - \mu t$.

Applying the principle of conservation of momentum:

At time t At time $t + dt$

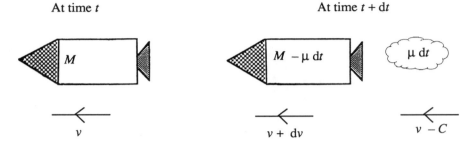

Total momentum at time t = Total momentum at time $t + dt$

$$Mv \approx (M - \mu\, dt)(v + dv) + \mu\, dt\, (v - C)$$
$$\Rightarrow \quad 0 \approx Mdv - \mu\, dt\, dv - \mu\, dt\, C$$

Since $dt\, dv$ is very small compared to other terms it can be ignored, giving:

$$0 \approx Mdv - \mu\, dtC$$

Dividing by dt :

$$M\frac{dv}{dt} - \mu C = 0 \text{ or } (M_0 - \mu t)\frac{dv}{dt} - \mu C = 0$$

where $\frac{dv}{dt}$ is the acceleration of the rocket and μ is the rate at which the fuel is ejected.

This equation of motion is known as the rocket equation. In this model μ and C have been assumed to be constant. Note that M is the mass of the spacecraft at time t and so is not constant.

> **Show that if $v = 0$ when $t = 0$, then**
>
> $$v = C \ln \left| \frac{M_0}{M_0 - \mu t} \right| . \text{ Interpret this solution.}$$

A similar equation can also be derived for a rocket taking off from the Earth.

TASKSHEET 3 – *Modelling rocket motion*

> You can obtain a model for the motion of a rocket by considering the change of momentum of the rocket and fuel in a time interval $(t, t + dt)$.
>
> In deep space the total rate of change of momentum is zero. In general, the total rate of change of momentum equals the resultant external force.

Example 2

An astronaut with a rocket pack is moving from a satellite back to his spacecraft at a speed of 2 ms⁻¹. He fires the rockets for 5 seconds. The gas from the pack has an exhaust speed of 30 ms⁻¹ and the fuel is burnt at a rate of 10 kg s⁻¹. Initially, the total mass of the astronaut and pack is 200 kg.

(a) Show that the equation of motion for the astronaut is:

$$(20 - t)\frac{dv}{dt} = 30$$

(b) Calculate the speed of the astronaut after 5 seconds.

(c) Sketch a graph of v against t.

Solution

(a) At time t .... At time $t + dt$

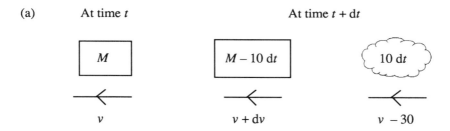

Using the principle of conservation of momentum:

$$Mv = (M - 10\,dt)(v + dv) + 10\,dt\,(v - 30)$$

$$\Rightarrow \quad 0 = Mdv - 10\,dt\,dv - 300\,dt$$

Ignoring $dt\,dv$ and dividing by dt:

$$M\frac{dv}{dt} = 300 \text{ and } M = 200 - 10t$$

$$\Rightarrow \quad (200 - 10t)\frac{dv}{dt} = 300$$

$$\Rightarrow \quad (20 - t)\frac{dv}{dt} = 30$$

(b) Separating variables:

$$\int_{2}^{v} dv = \int_{0}^{t} \frac{30}{20-t}\, dt$$

$$\Rightarrow v - 2 = -30 \ln \left| \frac{20-t}{20} \right|$$

$$\Rightarrow \quad v = 2 - 30 \ln \left| \frac{20-t}{20} \right|$$

Then $t = 5 \Rightarrow v = 10.63$

The speed of the astronaut at the end of the thrust is 10.6 ms^{-1} (to 3 s.f.).

(c)

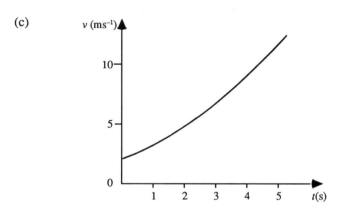

Exercise 2

(Assume $g = 10 \text{ ms}^{-2}$ and ignore air resistance, unless otherwise stated.)

1. For the astronaut in Example 2, explain what happens at $t = 20$.

2. A spacecraft is travelling initially at 250 ms^{-1} in outer space. As the spacecraft approaches a space station its reverse thrust rockets are fired. The rockets eject fuel at 1000 ms^{-1} relative to the craft and at a rate of 200 kg s^{-1}. Assume the attraction of the space station and other bodies to be negligible.

    (a) Let M kilograms be the mass of the spacecraft at time t. Using the principle of conservation of momentum, show that:

    $$M\frac{dv}{dt} = -200\,000$$

    (b) If initially the mass of the spacecraft is 9000 kg, show that the equation of motion for the spacecraft can be written as:

    $$(9000 - 200t)\frac{dv}{dt} = -200\,000$$

    (c) Calculate the time taken for the spacecraft to stop.

3. A rocket of initial mass 10 000 kg is launched vertically upwards under gravity. The rate at which the rocket burns fuel is 50 kg s^{-1} and the burnt matter is ejected vertically downwards with a speed of 2000 ms^{-1} relative to the rocket. The burning ends after three minutes.

   (a) Find the mass M kg of the rocket t seconds after the launch.

   (b) The equation of motion for the rocket is:

   $$M \frac{dv}{dt} = -Mg + 100\ 000$$

   Calculate the speed of the rocket after three minutes.

4. The motion of a rocket during lift-off is modelled by the equation:

   $$M \frac{dv}{dt} - \mu C = -9.8M - kv^2$$

   where C ms^{-1} is the speed of the exhaust gas relative to the rocket, μ kg s^{-1} is the rate of decrease in mass of the rocket, M kilograms is the mass of the rocket at time t seconds and k is a constant.

   (a) Describe the assumptions on which this model is based.

   (b) Give two reasons why this model would only be valid for the launch stage of the rocket's motion.

5. A lunar lander of initial mass 1.8×10^4 kg fires its rockets to lift off from the Moon. The rockets burn fuel at a steady rate of 180 kg s^{-1}. If the exhaust gas is ejected at 150 ms^{-1} relative to the lander, calculate the time taken before the lander begins to lift off.

3.4   Varying mass

There are other practical situations, similar to some you have already met in *Newton's laws of motion* and *Modelling with force and motion* where variable weight can be modelled and analysed.

> **(a)** How does the rate of ascent of the balloon change as sand, used as ballast, is poured over the side?
>
> **(b)** Describe the possible motion of the trolley on the slope if the bucket of water is leaking.
>
> **(c)** What happens to the motion of the masses in the 'Bricklayer's lament' if a heavy chain is used instead of string?

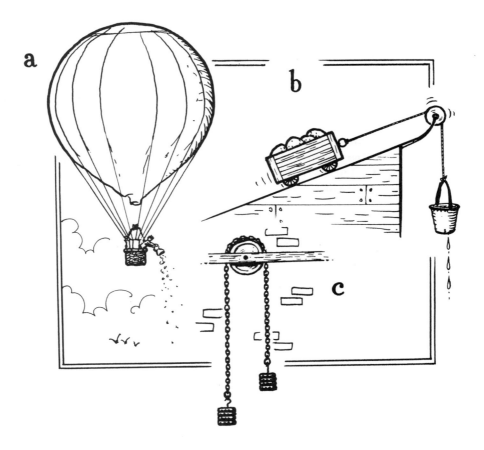

These three examples could be modelled using the methods of this chapter and (b) and (c) could be investigated practically. Other situations contained in this chapter could also form the basis of an extended investigation.

After working through this chapter you should:

1.   be able to model the motion of bodies subject to a variable gravitational force;

2.   know what is meant by the term escape speed and be able to calculate it;

3.   be able to model the motion of a body of variable mass such as a rocket;

4.   be able to solve differential equations of the form:

$$v \frac{dv}{dx} = f(x) \quad \text{or} \quad \frac{dv}{dt} = f(t) \, ;$$

5.   be able to interpret graphical, analytical and numerical solutions to problems in variable weight and variable mass contexts.

The Moon-lander

The Moon-lander has run out of fuel at a height of 50 km above the surface.

 Problem   What is the speed on impact when it crash lands?

Assume that the only force acting on the lander is its weight, which varies according to Newton's law of gravitation.

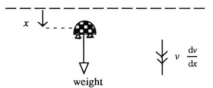

1.   Show that the equation of motion for the lander of mass m kilograms can be written as:

$$mv \frac{dv}{dx} = \frac{GMm}{(R + 50\,000 - x)^2}$$

where v ms^{-1} is the speed of descent after falling a distance x metres, M kilograms is the mass and R metres is the radius of the Moon.

2.   Find an expression for the speed in terms of x, with initial conditions $v = 0$ and $x = 0$.

3.   Calculate the impact speed of the lander.

4.   Compare this value for the impact speed with the value calculated at the beginning of this chapter using a constant gravity model.

5.   Show that a general expression for the impact speed V_h for an object falling from height h metres above the surface is

$$V_h = \sqrt{\left(\frac{2GMh}{R(R+h)}\right)}$$

6.   (a)   Sketch a graph of impact speed V_h against height h over the range $0 < h < 20\,000\,000$. Describe how the variation in weight affects the descent of the lander.

       (b)   Superimpose the graph of impact speed calculated under the assumption of constant gravity, $g_m = 1.62$ ms^{-2}. Comment on the difference between the two graphs.

7E.   Show that $V_h \approx \left(1 - \frac{h}{2R}\right)\sqrt{(2g_m h)}$ for an appropriate range of values of h.

Rocket propulsion

Imagine standing on a trolley or a skateboard with a large bag of heavy balls. Suppose there is very little friction acting on the wheels of the trolley.

1.   What will happen when a ball is thrown off the trolley?

2.   Describe the effect each of the following will have on the trolley's motion:

   (a)   the speed at which each ball is thrown;

   (b)   the mass of each ball and the mass of the trolley;

   (c)   the rate at which the balls are thrown.

It may be possible for you to verify some of these ideas if you have suitable equipment. You can set up a mathematical model for this motion by making some assumptions about the speeds and masses involved.

Set up a model

The assumptions:
- the mass of you and your trolley is 60 kg;
- the mass of each ball is 2 kg;
- the speed of the balls is 10 ms^{-1} (relative to the trolley);
- the throwing rate is 1 per second;
- the initial number of balls is 100;
- the initial speed of the trolley is 0 ms^{-1};
- the speed of trolley at time t is v ms^{-1}.
- the air resistance and friction are negligible.

(continued)

Analyse the problem

3. Draw momentum diagrams before and after one ball has been projected.

4. Applying the principle of conservation of momentum to the trolley and the ball, show that the speed of the trolley after one ball has been thrown off (i.e. after one second) is $\frac{10}{129}$ ms^{-1}.

5. Find the speed of the trolley over the next three seconds. [Note that when the trolley is moving forwards with speed v, the actual forwards speed of the ball relative to the ground is $v - 10$ ms^{-1}.]

It is possible to generalise the situation to calculate these small increases in speed using an iterative sequence.

6. Consider a trolley moving with initial speed v_0 ms^{-1}. The trolley has mass M kilograms and carries 100 balls, each of mass m kilograms. The balls are thrown from the trolley at a speed of C ms^{-1} relative to the trolley, at a rate of 1 per second. Let v_n ms^{-1} be the speed of the trolley after n balls have been thrown.

   (a) Show that $v_1 = v_0 + \frac{mC}{M + 99m}$

   (b) Find a similar expression for v_2 in terms of v_1.

   (c) Find an expression for v_n in terms of v_{n-1}.

7. Use your answers to question 6 to check your solutions to question 5.

8. v_n can be expressed as the sum of the sequence:

$$v_n = \frac{mC}{M + (100-n).m} + \ldots\ldots + \frac{mC}{M + 97m} + \frac{mC}{M + 98m} + \frac{mC}{M + 99m}.$$

   Using a program, calculate the speed of the original trolley after each 10 throws, plot the graph of speed against time for the trolley's motion and write down the final speed after 100 throws.

9E. State the effect on the motion of the trolley of increasing:

   (a) the mass of the balls;

   (b) the speed of the throw;

   (c) the throwing rate.

Modelling rocket motion

 Problem Find the differential equation of motion for a rocket lifting off from the Earth

To analyse the motion, consider the changes in mass and velocity over a short interval of time dt.

The diagrams show the rocket and the exhaust gas ejected in the time interval of dt. M is the mass of the rocket at time t, μ dt is the mass of the ejected gas and C is the speed of the exhaust gas relative to the rocket.

(continued)

1. At the start of the time interval the rocket and exhaust gas have total mass M and velocity v and so have momentum Mv.

    (a) Find the total momentum of the rocket and exhaust gas at the end of the time interval. Simplify your answer.

    (b) Find the change in momentum during the time interval. By dividing by dt, show that the rate of change of momentum is:

    $$M \frac{dv}{dt} - \mu C$$

2. Explain why the total external force acting on the rocket and exhaust gas is constant during the time interval. Hence show that the equation of motion for the rocket is:

    $$M \frac{dv}{dt} - \mu C = - Mg$$

3. In the diagram, T is the magnitude of the thrust on the rocket, the interaction force between the rocket and the gas.

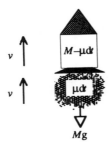

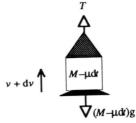

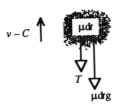

    By considering just the rate of change of momentum of the gas, show that:

    $$T = \mu C$$

4. What condition on μ, C and M must be satisfied in order for lift-off to actually take place?

5E. Show that if the initial mass of the rocket is M_0, where $M_0 \geq \frac{\mu C}{g}$, it will only lift-off after time τ where

    $$\tau = \frac{M_0}{\mu} - \frac{C}{g}$$

    Interpret this equation for (a) $\tau = 0$, (b) $\tau > 0$.

Tutorial sheet

1.   A rocket is launched from the Earth to take readings in the upper atmosphere. It is designed to travel to a height of 25 km.

The equation of motion for the rocket is

$$\frac{dv}{dt} = -10 + \frac{1250}{100 - t}$$

where v ms^{-1} is the speed of the rocket vertically upwards.

(a)   Find the initial acceleration of the rocket.

(b)   Draw a graph showing how the acceleration varies with time.

(c)   If the rocket has enough fuel for 80 seconds of thrust, calculate the speed of the rocket when the fuel runs out.

(d)   If this model was used to calculate the maximum height reached, give two reasons why the solution might be an over-estimate.

2.   A three stage rocket is launched at time $t = 0$. The graph shows how its speed varies with time.

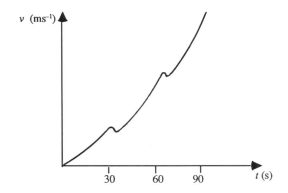

(a)   Explain what occurs at time (i) $t = 30$ seconds, (ii) $t = 35$ seconds.

(b)   Each of the three stages of the rocket has mass 1200 kg plus 3000 kg of fuel and is jettisoned when empty. In addition there is a command module of mass 1600 kg at the top of the rocket.

The fuel in each stage is burnt at a rate of 100 kg s^{-1} and is ejected at C ms^{-1} relative to the rocket. The equation of motion at the start of the first stage of thrust is

$$14\,200\,\frac{dv}{dt} = -142\,000 + 100C$$

Write down the equations of motion at the start of the second and third stages of thrust.

(continued)

3. A lunar module of mass 1200 kg together with 600 kg of fuel is descending towards the Moon. When travelling at 100 ms^{-1} vertically downwards the rockets are fired to slow the lander. The exhaust gas is ejected at 360 ms^{-1} at a rate of 50 kg s^{-1}.

The equation for the motion t seconds after the rockets are fired is:

$$M\frac{dv}{dt} = Mg - 18\,000$$

where M is the total mass of the module at time t and g = 1.62 ms^{-2} is assumed to be constant.

(a) Find an expression for M at time t.

(b) Integrate the equation of motion for the descent speed v at time t.

(c) Graphically, or otherwise, find the time taken for the module to slow to a zero descent speed.

4. In a model for the motion of a projectile fired from the surface of the Moon, the gravitational attraction is assumed to decrease linearly with the height, h metres, above the surface according to the relationship:

$$g_h = 1.62\,(1 - \frac{2h}{R})$$

where R is the radius of the Moon.

(a) Deduce an equation of motion for the projectile.

(b) Show that the launch speed U, in terms of the maximum height attained H, can be written as:

$$U = \sqrt{\left(3.24H\,(1 - \frac{H}{R})\right)}$$

(c) Comment on the validity of this model, in particular when H approaches R.

4 *Simple harmonic motion*

4.1 Vibrations everywhere

Vibrations and oscillations play a major part in everyday life. Everything you hear is vibrating! Some vibrations are useful, some are essential, some are irritating and some are even destructive.

> **(a)** List some examples where vibrations are beneficial, and some where they can be a disadvantage or even destructive.
>
> **(b)** What features of an oscillation can be measured?

In each vibration, a point can be identified which is moving about a fixed mean position, i.e. oscillating. For example, each point on the baby in the baby-bouncer is moving up and down about a mean position. Suitable functions to model this oscillating behaviour would be sine or cosine functions or a combination, such as

$$x = a \cos \omega t, \ x = a \sin \omega t \ \text{or} \ x = a \cos \omega t + b \sin \omega t,$$

where $a(t)$ is the amplitude of oscillation, which may grow, decay or be constant, and ω is the number of oscillations in 2π seconds, called the angular frequency.

The graph of $x = a \cos \omega t$ is as shown.

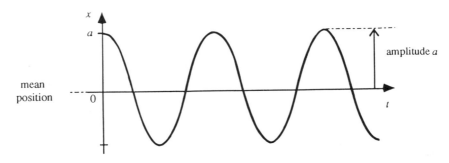

Example 1

A small child is placed in a baby-bouncer hung from a door frame. The height of the baby's bottom above the floor was measured as the baby bounced up and down. The results are plotted on the graph below.

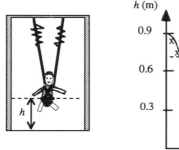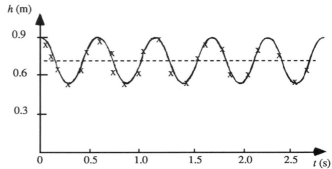

Describe the baby's motion:

(a)   in words   (b)   by a suitable function, $h(t)$.

Solution

(a)   The baby bounces up and down with a steady oscillation. In 2 seconds, approximately three and a half bounces are made, i.e. one bounce every 0.6 second. The baby's bottom reaches a maximum height of 0.9 metre and a lowest height of about 0.54 metre. The bounces seem to be all roughly the same amplitude.

(b)   A cosine function of the type $h = a \cos \omega t + C$ seems to fit the data quite well. The time for one oscillation is 0.6 second, so in 2π seconds there will the $\frac{2\pi}{0.6} = 10.5$ oscillations. Therefore ω is 10.5, the amplitude $a = 0.18$ and the mean position is at $h = 0.72$.

So a suitable function to model this data would be $h = 0.18 \cos (10.5t) + 0.72$.

> The fixed position about which a moving point oscillates is
> known as the mean or equilibrium position. The maximum
> displacement is called the amplitude, a.
>
> The time for one complete oscillation is called the time period, τ.
>
> The number of oscillations in 2π seconds is called the angular
> frequency, ω, and so $\tau = \frac{2\pi}{\omega}$.

Exercise 1

1. Describe in words the motion in the following situations represented by the
   graphs, giving the time period and amplitude of oscillation. Suggest suitable
   functions for the graphs. In each case, $x(t)$ is the vertical displacement of an
   appropriate point.

   (a) A seagull on the sea.

   (b) A spin-drier with an uneven load.

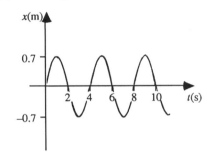
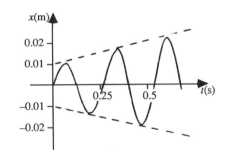

2. A piston is moving back and forth in a cylinder as shown in the diagram below.

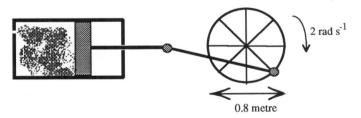

   (a) Sketch a graph representing the motion of a point in the piston's plunger
   over a suitable period of time.

   (b) Suggest a possible function for your graph.

3. Hold a ruler over the edge of a table and
   strike it so that it vibrates. Try to model
   the vibration with a suitable function.

57

4.2   Simple harmonic motion

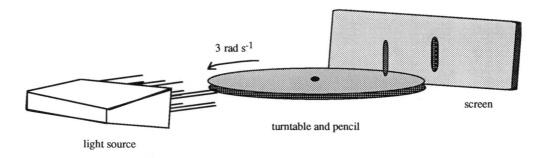

3 rad s⁻¹

screen

turntable and pencil

light source

Consider the situation above. The pencil is fixed 20 cm from the centre of a turntable, rotating with constant angular speed 3 rad s⁻¹. The light projects the pencil's shadow onto a vertical screen.

> **(a)**   **Describe how the shadow moves.**
>
> **(b)**   **Model its displacement with a graph and suggest a suitable function.**

A general model can be set up to describe the motion of the shadow.

Plan view:

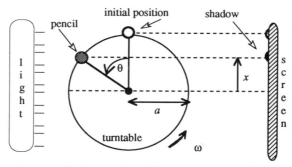

Assume that the turntable is rotating with a constant angular speed of ω rad s⁻¹. The pencil is fixed at a distance a metres from the axis. Assume the timing begins when the pencil's shadow is at its extreme position on the screen.

Let θ radians be the angle of displacement of the pencil at time t seconds and let x metres be the corresponding displacement of the shadow from the mean (central) position.

From the diagram, $x = a \cos \theta$.

The initial angle of displacement is zero (i.e. when $t = 0$, $\theta = 0$) $\Rightarrow \theta = \omega t$.

So the position of the shadow is given by $x = a \cos \omega t$.

The graph shows the shadow's displacement, x metres, with time, t seconds.

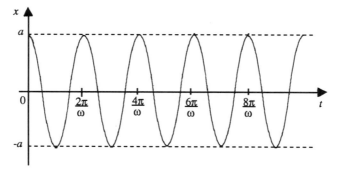

From the graph, the time period $\tau = \dfrac{2\pi}{\omega}$.

You may have already seen cosine and sine functions referred to as harmonic functions. Accordingly, the shadow's motion is an example of **simple harmonic motion, SHM**.

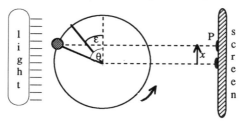

For general initial conditions, for example when $t = 0$, $\theta = \varepsilon$, then $\theta = \omega t + \varepsilon$.

The motion of the shadow is still called simple harmonic and the function describing its displacement is of the form:

$$x = a \cos (\omega t + \varepsilon)$$

where a is the amplitude, ω is the angular frequency of oscillation and ε is a constant called the **phase constant.**

> **Show that $a \cos (\omega t + \varepsilon)$ is equivalent to $A \cos \omega t + B \sin \omega t$ and express the arbitrary constants A and B in terms of a and ε.**

In general the displacement, velocity and acceleration of a body performing simple harmonic motion are given by;

•	displacement	$x = a \cos (\omega t + \varepsilon)$	①
•	velocity	$\dot{x} = -a \omega \sin (\omega t + \varepsilon)$	②
•	acceleration	$\ddot{x} = -a\omega^2 \cos (\omega t + \varepsilon)$	③

Comparing equations ① and ③:

$$\frac{d^2 x}{dt^2} = -\omega^2 x$$

The defining characteristic of simple harmonic motion is that the acceleration is proportional to the displacement of the body from the mean position, though it is always directed towards the mean position.

> **The equation for simple harmonic motion is :**
> $$\ddot{x} + \omega^2 x = 0$$
>
> **This has the general solution:**
>
> $$x = a \cos (\omega t + \varepsilon) \text{ or } x = A \cos \omega t + B \sin \omega t$$
>
> **where a, ε, A and B are arbitrary constants determined by the initial conditions.**

Exercise 2

1. The displacement from the mean position of the shadow of a rotating pencil is given by $x = 0.2 \cos 3t$.

   (a) Sketch, on the same set of axes, the graphs for the shadow's displacement, velocity and acceleration against time, for $0 \le t \le 12$ seconds.

   (b) From the graphs, find the displacement of the shadow when:

   (i) its acceleration is zero; (ii) its acceleration is maximum;

   (iii) its velocity is zero; (iv) its velocity is maximum.

2. Show by substitution that the model for the baby-bouncer, $x = 0.18 \cos (10.5t)$, satisfies the SHM equation, $\ddot{x} + \omega^2 x = 0$, for some value of ω. (Note that in this case x is the displacement from the mean position.)

3. Find the displacement, x, of the pencil's shadow, P, as a function of t given that P is at I when $t = 0$.

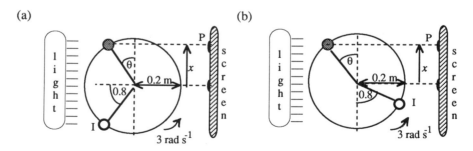

   (a)   (b)

4. Show by substitution that $x = A \cos \omega t + B \sin \omega t$ is a general solution to the SHM equation:
   $$\frac{d^2 x}{dt^2} + \omega^2 x = 0$$

60

4.3 Modelling an oscillating body

Collecting data from oscillating bodies makes it possible to find a function that models the motion, as in the example of the baby-bouncer. However, this does not give any insight into how the bouncer would behave when a heavier or lighter baby uses it. To design a bouncer suitable for a range of different sized babies, an understanding of how the mass of the baby influences the period and amplitude of oscillation is needed.

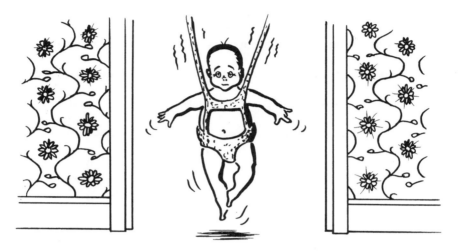

 Problem   How does the period of oscillation of the baby-bouncer vary with the mass of the baby?

To set up a differential equation you will need to apply Newton's second law. This requires a model for the forces involved.

Using a spring or string with different loads, investigate the following questions.

(a) **What effect does the magnitude of the initial displacement have on the time period of oscillation?**

(b) **For how many oscillations can the amplitude be assumed to be constant?**

(c) **Comment on the validity of Hooke's law as a model for the tension in the spring or string throughout the motion. (Consider the case where the spring is in compression or where the string becomes slack.)**

(d) **What other assumptions need to be made to set up a model?**

Simplify the bouncer to a single spring of natural length l metres. Assume the tension in the spring can be modelled by Hooke's law. Assume also that the baby is a particle of mass m kilograms suspended from the spring so that it is never in contact with the floor. Ignore air resistance.

When in equilibrium the spring is extended by a length, e metres. The baby is pulled down a further a metres and released.

Let x metres be the displacement of the baby beyond the equilibrium position at time t.

There are three positions to consider, as shown in the diagram below.

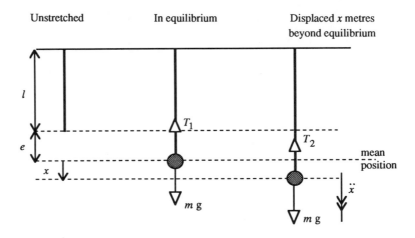

Analyse the problem

In the equilibrium position, $mg = T_1$
and from Hooke's law, $T_1 = ke$

$\Rightarrow$ $mg = ke$

For a further vertical displacement, x, the new tension is $T_2 = k(e + x)$. There will be a resultant force, $mg - T_2$. So using Newton's second law vertically downwards:

$$mg - k(e + x) = m\ddot{x}$$

Substituting $mg = ke$:

$$-kx = m\ddot{x} \quad \Rightarrow \ddot{x} = -\frac{k}{m}x$$

This differential equation is the same as the equation for SHM (in Section 4.2):

$$\ddot{x} = -\omega^2 x$$

where the angular frequency, $\omega = \sqrt{\left(\frac{k}{m}\right)}$.

(a)   For the baby-bouncer, use the initial conditions $t = 0$, $x = a$ and $\frac{dx}{dt} = 0$ to show that the solution to the differential equation is

$$x = a \cos \sqrt{\left(\frac{k}{m}\right)}\, t$$

(b)   For $k = 500$, $m = 10$ and $a = 0.6$, sketch the graph of the displacement x against time t for the oscillating baby.

(c)   Use the graph to estimate the time period of oscillation.

Interpret/validate

The initial problem was to find how the time period of oscillation varies with the mass of the baby. Using the graph it is possible to find the time period τ.

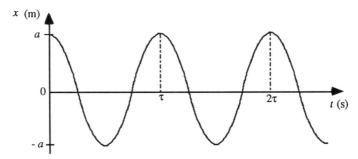

The first oscillation is complete when $t = \tau \Rightarrow \cos\left(\sqrt{\left(\frac{k}{m}\right)}\tau\right) = 1$

i.e. when $\sqrt{\left(\frac{k}{m}\right)}\tau = 2\pi$

So the time period of one oscillation is:

$$\tau = \frac{2\pi}{\sqrt{\left(\frac{k}{m}\right)}} = 2\pi\sqrt{\left(\frac{m}{k}\right)}$$

(Alternatively, the formula $\tau = \frac{2\pi}{\omega}$ where $\omega = \sqrt{\left(\frac{k}{m}\right)}$ can be used to give this result.)

Interpret this formula. What does it tell you about the time period of oscillation for different masses and different strings or springs?

It should now be possible to validate the solution with data from an experiment using different masses on strings and springs, or even a real baby in a baby-bouncer.

TASKSHEET 1 – *Validating the formula T $\propto\sqrt{m}$*

63

Example 2

A metal block of mass 2 kg is attached to the end of a light spring of natural length 30 cm. The other end is fixed to a wall and the whole system is at rest on a smooth horizontal table, with the spring unstretched.

The block is struck so that it moves away from the wall with an initial speed of 2 ms⁻¹. Assume the spring obeys Hooke's law (i.e. it is a Hookean spring) and has a spring constant of 800 Nm⁻¹.

(a)   Show that the equation of motion can be written as $\dfrac{d^2x}{dt^2} = -400x$

where x metres is the displacement of the block from its original position.

(b)   Solve the equation for the displacement in terms of time, t.

(c)   How close does the block get to the wall during the subsequent motion?

Solution

(a)   Assume that the block is a particle, the air resistance is negligible and the spring obeys Hooke's law for the whole motion.

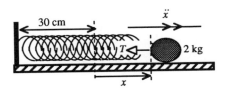

Using Newton's second law: $m\dfrac{d^2x}{dt^2} = -T$

From Hooke's law: $T = 800x$

$$\Rightarrow\ 2\frac{d^2x}{dt^2} = -800x \ \Rightarrow\ \frac{d^2x}{dt^2} = -400x$$

(b)   This is an equation for SHM which has a solution in the form $x = a \cos(\omega t + \varepsilon)$, where $\omega^2 = 400$.

From the equation, $\omega = 20$. The initial conditions are $t = 0$, $x = 0$, $\dot{x} = 2$, so

$$x = a \cos \varepsilon = 0 \Rightarrow \varepsilon = \frac{\pi}{2}$$

Substituting ω and ε in the general solution gives $x = a \cos(20t + \frac{\pi}{2})$ or $x = -a \sin(20t)$.

Differentiating for velocity, $\dot{x} = -20\, a \cos(20t)$

When $t = 0$, $\dot{x} = 2$, so $2 = -20\, a \cos 0 \Rightarrow a = -0.1$

Therefore the displacement of the block is $x = 0.1 \sin 20t$.

(c)   The amplitude is 0.1 metre, so the closest the block gets to the wall is 20 cm.

Exercise 3   (Take g = 10 ms^{-2}.)

1.   A bob suspended on an elastic string is released from an initial displacement of 1.0 cm below its equilibrium position. The displacement from equilibrium of the bob, x metres, is given by a function of the form $x = a \cos \omega t$. The time for 10 oscillations is 8 seconds.

     (a)   Show that $a = \dfrac{1}{100}$ and $\omega = \dfrac{5\pi}{2}$.

     (b)   Calculate the maximum speed and maximum acceleration of the bob.

     (c)   State the displacement of the bob when these maxima occur.

2.   A Hookean spring of natural length 30 cm doubles in length when a 100 g mass is hung on the end of it.

     (a)   Find a formula for the tension in the spring.

     From the equilibrium position, the hanging mass is displaced a further 2 cm downwards and released so that it oscillates vertically.

     (b)   Calculate the initial acceleration of the mass.

     (c)   Find the time period of these small oscillations.

3.   A particle of mass 3 kg is suspended from a vertical Hookean spring of length 6 metres and spring constant 15 Nm^{-1}. The particle is pulled down until the spring is 9 metres long and then released from rest.

     (a)   Show that the equation of motion is:

     $$\frac{d^2x}{dt^2} = 10 - 5x$$

     where x metres is the extension of the spring.

     (b)   Verify by substitution that $x = 2 + \cos \sqrt{5}\, t$ is a solution to the differential equation.

     (c)   Show that the spring never actually compresses.

4.   A particle of mass 1.2 kg is attached between two identical Hookean springs which rest on a smooth horizontal table. The other end of each spring is fixed to a support. The springs are unstretched until the particle is displaced to one side and then released.

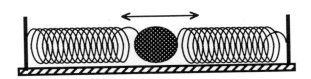

(a) Assuming that air resistance and friction are negligible, draw a diagram showing the forces on the particle when its displacement is x metres from the central position.

(b) If the spring constant of both springs is 24 Nm^{-1}, write down the equation of motion of the particle and show that it performs SHM with angular frequency of 6.32 rad s^{-1}.

The SHM equation is an example of a second order differential equation and can be solved by various methods without reference to the general solution. Tasksheet 2E demonstrates other methods of solution of the SHM equation.

TASKSHEET 2E – *Solving the SHM equation*

After working through this chapter you should:

1. understand and be able to use the terms equilibrium or mean position, amplitude, time period and angular frequency when applied to oscillations;

2. be able to recognise the equation for simple harmonic motion $\ddot{x} + \omega^2 x = 0$, and write down its general solution;

3. be able to model the motion of a body oscillating on the end of a spring by applying Hooke's law;

4. be able to interpret solutions to the SHM equation.

Validating the formula $T \propto \sqrt{m}$

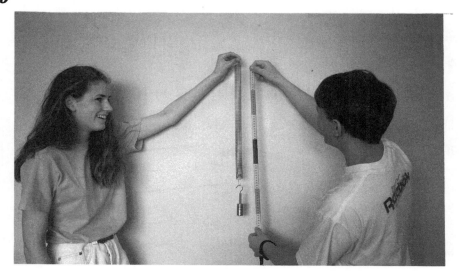

The objective is to validate the formula for a real spring.

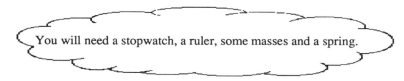

You will need a stopwatch, a ruler, some masses and a spring.

Before starting to take any measurements it is advisable initially to stretch the springs a few times to loosen them up. Take care not to overstretch the springs as this may cause them to break, or more likely to deform.

1.   Find the spring constant k of your spring, assuming that Hooke's law is valid.

2.   Measure the time period for a suitable range of masses.

3.   By plotting a graph of the time period, τ seconds against the mass m kilograms, comment on the validity of the formula $\tau \propto \sqrt{m}$. Also comment on the validity of the specific solution

$$T = \frac{2\pi}{\sqrt{(\frac{k}{m})}} = 2\pi \sqrt{(\frac{m}{k})}$$

using the value of k found previously.

Solving the SHM equation

The equation for simple harmonic motion is the second order differential equation $\ddot{x} = -\omega^2 x$.

Method A — Separation of variables

1. An alternative form of the SHM equation is $v \dfrac{dv}{dx} + \omega^2 x = 0$, where $v = \dot{x}$.

   Show, by separation of variables, that this has a solution $v^2 = -\omega^2 x^2 + \text{constant}$.

2. If the initial conditions are $x = a$ and $v = 0$, then show that

$$v = \pm \omega \sqrt{(a^2 - x^2)}$$

3. Sketch a graph of velocity against displacement and interpret it as x varies from $-a$ to a.

4. Show that separating variables once again gives,

$$\int_{0}^{t} dt = \int_{a}^{x} \frac{\pm 1}{\omega \sqrt{(a^2 - x^2)}} \, dx$$

   and find a solution for $x\,(t)$.

5. The equation of motion for the mass on a spring is

$$\ddot{x} = -\frac{k}{m} x$$

   Find the solution for the initial conditions $t = 0$, $x = 0$, $\dot{x} = 9$. Suggest a possible physical situation that would have these initial conditions.

Method B — Auxiliary equation

6. Substituting $x = A\,e^{pt}$ in the differential equation $\ddot{x} + \omega^2 x = 0$, obtain the auxiliary equation $p^2 + \omega^2 = 0$.

7. Show that the differential equation has a general solution $x = A\,e^{j\omega t} + B\,e^{-j\omega t}$ where $j = \sqrt{-1}$, and A, B are arbitrary constants.

8. Use the relationship $e^{j\theta} = (\cos\theta + j\sin\theta)$ to write the general solution in the form

$$x = P\cos\omega t + Q\sin\omega t.$$

   Thus the complex solution, $x = A\,e^{j\omega t} + B\,e^{-j\omega t}$, to the differential equation can be written as a real trigonometric function $x = P\cos\omega t + Q\sin\omega t$, where P and Q are a pair of arbitrary constants obtained from the initial conditions.

1. The height, h metres, of a boat's deck above the quay in a harbour varies with time, t seconds, as the tide comes in and goes out according to

$$h = 0.6 - 0.4 \cos\left(\frac{\pi t}{22\,000} + \frac{\pi}{2}\right)$$

   (a) Deduce an expression for the displacement, x metres, from the mean position.

   (b) Show, by substitution, that the motion of the deck is simple harmonic, i.e. $\ddot{x} + \omega^2 x = 0$, where ω is a constant.

   (c) If $t = 0$ at midnight, find the time of the following high tide.

2. A particle is oscillating so that its displacement x metres at time t seconds is given by

$$x = 0.9 \sin\left(\frac{\pi t}{3} + \frac{\pi}{12}\right)$$

   (a) Find the number of oscillations per second.

   (b) Calculate the maximum acceleration and the time, after $t = 0$, that it first occurs.

3.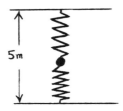
   Two identical Hookean springs of natural length 1.0 m are fixed so that they hang vertically with a particle of mass 0.6 kg attached between them. The other ends of the springs are attached to two points 5.0 m apart. The spring constant of the springs is 20 Nm^{-1}. Initially the particle is pulled a short distance below the equilibrium position and then released.

   (a) Calculate the displacement of the equilibrium position below the upper fixed point.

   (b) If x metres is the displacement of the particle from equilibrium after t seconds, derive an equation in x and t for the subsequent motion of the particle. Deduce the angular frequency of the oscillations.

4. The top of a flag pole is free to sway in the wind. A single strong gust of wind gives the top an initial displacement of 1.2m from the vertical. Subsequently the top moves back and forth in an approximately horizontal plane and the motion is modelled by:

$$\frac{d^2 x}{dt^2} + 16\pi^2 x = 0$$

   Solve this equation for the displacement x metres at time t seconds. Suggest a reason why this model gives an unrealistic solution.

5 *Other oscillations*

5.1 The pendulum

The first pendulum clock was invented in about 1657 by Christiaan Huygens. Up until the 1950s the most accurate clocks were pendulum clocks, the best being accurate to within a few thousandths of a second per day. To ensure such accuracy it is essential to know how to modify the period of oscillation.

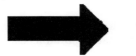

TASKSHEET 1 – *Pendulum clocks*

In the tasksheet, the effects of three factors on the time period were considered – the length, the mass of the bob and the amplitude. Before studying the theoretical analysis you should be familiar with the result that the tangential component of acceleration of a particle moving in a circle of radius r is $r\ddot{\theta}$. This was established in the unit *Modelling with circular motion* and is repeated on Tasksheet 2S.

TASKSHEET 2S – *Calculating acceleration*

Problem How is the time period of oscillation of a pendulum affected by varying the length, mass or amplitude?

Set up a model

To analyse the motion of a pendulum, a simple model is required. Assume that the pendulum consists of a bob on the end of an inextensible string or rod. The bob is assumed to be a particle of mass m kilograms and the string or rod is assumed to have no mass. The other end of the string is suspended from a fixed point so that the pendulum swings freely. The friction at the pivot and air resistance are assumed to be negligible. This is known as a **simple pendulum.**

Assume that the simple pendulum is of length l metres. Let it be displaced initially by a small angle, α radians, from the vertical, and then released. Let θ radians be the angle the string makes with the vertical at time t seconds.

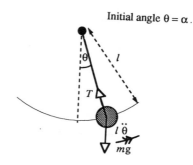

Initial angle $\theta = \alpha$.

Analyse the problem

Using Newton's second law, taking the component along the tangent to the arc in the direction of increasing θ:

$$-mg \sin \theta = ml \frac{d^2\theta}{dt^2}$$

$$\ddot{\theta} = -\frac{g}{l} \sin \theta$$

Notice that m cancels out and so does not affect the rest of the analysis (i.e. the motion is independent of the mass of the bob).

If the angle of displacement is small then the approximation $\sin \theta \approx \theta$ can be made. So the equation of motion becomes:

$$\ddot{\theta} = -\frac{g}{l}\theta$$

This is the SHM equation, with $\omega^2 = \frac{g}{l}$. The general solution is:

$$\theta = a \cos\left(t\sqrt{\left(\frac{g}{l}\right)} + \varepsilon\right)$$

where a and ε are constants determined by the initial conditions. In this example, $\theta = \alpha$ and $\dot{\theta} = 0$ when $t = 0$ and so

$$\theta = \alpha \cos\left(t\sqrt{\left(\frac{g}{l}\right)}\right)$$

71

The time period is given by:

$$\tau = \frac{2\pi}{\omega} = 2\pi \sqrt{\left(\frac{l}{g}\right)}$$

τ is independent of the mass of the bob and depends only on the length of the pendulum and the value of g. For a pendulum of length 1 metre, i.e. $l = 1$ and $g = 10$, the time period is $2\pi\sqrt{\left(\frac{1}{10}\right)} \approx 2.0$ seconds.

> **Explain how you should vary l to correct a pendulum clock which runs fast or slow.**

This model implies the time period is independent of the amplitude. However, experimental results suggest that this is not the case for larger amplitudes. In setting up the model it was assumed that the amplitude was small, which allowed the small angle approximation $\sin \theta \approx \theta$ to be made. The pendulum equation $\ddot{\theta} = -\frac{g}{l} \sin \theta$ can be solved numerically by an Euler step method using

$$\theta_{n+1} = \theta_n + \dot{\theta}_n \, dt \;,\; \dot{\theta}_{n+1} = \dot{\theta}_n + \ddot{\theta}_n \, dt \text{ and } \ddot{\theta}_{n+1} = -\frac{g}{l} \sin \theta_n$$

> (a) For $l = 1$, $g = 10$ and $\alpha = 0.1$, use a time interval of 0.01 to find the time period of the pendulum.
>
> (b) Find the time period if α is changed to 1.5

> The motion of a simple pendulum of length l metres, for small amplitude oscillations, can be modelled as simple harmonic motion, i.e. $\ddot{\theta} + \omega^2\theta = 0$, where $\omega = \sqrt{\left(\frac{g}{l}\right)}$.
>
> However, for larger amplitude oscillations the pendulum equation should be used:
>
> $$\ddot{\theta} + \frac{g}{l} \sin \theta = 0$$

Example 1

The equation of motion of a pendulum, consisting of a bar with a slide weight is $\ddot{\theta} + 0.64 \sin \theta = 0$, where θ radians is the displacement of the bar from the vertical. The pendulum is released from rest with an initial angle of displacement 0.1 radian.

(a) Find an expression for its subsequent displacement in terms of time t seconds.

(b) Calculate the approximate number of oscillations performed in one minute.

Solution

(a)   Since the angle of displacement is small, the equation of motion becomes
$\ddot\theta + 0.64\theta = 0$.

This is the SHM equation where $\omega = \sqrt{0.64} = 0.8$.

Therefore the general solution is $\theta = a \cos (0.8t + \varepsilon)$.

The initial conditions are $t = 0$, $\theta = 0.1 \Rightarrow 0.1 = a \cos \varepsilon$ ①

Differentiating for angular velocity:

$$\dot\theta = -0.8\, a \sin (0.8t + \varepsilon)$$

Initially, $\dot\theta = 0 \Rightarrow 0 = -0.8\, a \sin \varepsilon \Rightarrow \sin \varepsilon = 0 \Rightarrow \varepsilon = 0$.

Substituting in ① gives $a = 0.1$.

So the angular displacement of the bar is $\theta = 0.1 \cos (0.8t)$.

(b)   The time period, $\tau = \frac{2\pi}{0.8} = 7.85$ seconds. So in 60 seconds there will be
approximately seven and a half oscillations.

Exercise 1 (Take g = 10 ms^{-2}.)

1.   A simple pendulum is hanging vertically at rest, when it is gently struck and given
an initial angular velocity of 0.2 rad s^{-1}. The subsequent motion is described by
the differential equation:

$$\frac{d^2\theta}{dt^2} + \frac{25}{9}\theta = 0$$

where θ radians is the angle the string makes with the vertical.

(a)   Solve the equation of motion giving θ as a function of time, t seconds.

(b)   Find the time period of the oscillations.

(c)   State three main assumptions that have been made in setting up the
differential equation.

2.   A simple pendulum with a bob of mass 200 grams is displaced initially by an
angle of 0.17 radian and released. The subsequent oscillations have a time period
of 0.9 second.

(a)   Estimate the length of the pendulum.

(b)   Find the maximum angular speed of the bob.

3.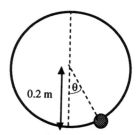

0.2 m

A smooth circular ring of wire of radius 0.2 metre, is fixed in a vertical plane with a small bead of mass 15 grams threaded onto the wire, as shown in the diagram.

The bead oscillates to and fro about the lowest position.

(a) Set up a model for the motion of the bead, drawing a diagram of the forces acting on the bead when in the position shown in the diagram.

(b) Assuming that the amplitude of oscillation is small, show that the equation of motion is:

$$\frac{d^2\theta}{dt^2} + 50\theta = 0$$

(c) Deduce the time period of oscillation of the bead.

4. (a) By differentiating the equation:

$$\dot{\theta}^2 = \frac{2g}{l}\cos\theta + C, \text{ where } C \text{ is constant}$$

verify that:

$$\dot{\theta} = \pm \sqrt{\left(\frac{2g}{l}\cos\theta + C\right)}$$

is a general solution to the pendulum equation, $\ddot{\theta} + \frac{g}{l}\sin\theta = 0$.

(b) For a simple pendulum of length 1 metre, released from rest when $\theta = \frac{\pi}{2}$ radians, show that the solution for $\dot{\theta}$ is:

$$\dot{\theta} = \pm\sqrt{(20\cos\theta)}$$

(c) Explain why the time period of oscillation is:

$$4\int_{0}^{\pi/2} \frac{d\theta}{\sqrt{(20\cos\theta)}}$$

Use a numerical method to evaluate this integral and compare your answer with the time period for oscillations of small amplitude.

5.2   Damping

So far, in setting up the model for the motion of an oscillating body the amplitude has been assumed to be constant. In reality, this may only be valid for a short time. For example, the amplitude of oscillation of a mass on the end of a spring gradually decreases. This is an example of **damping**.

In many systems damping is deliberately introduced to reduce unwanted vibrations. Examples are the shock absorbers in a vehicle's suspension, damped restoring springs in doors and dash-pots in gauges and meters to stop the needles or pointers oscillating.

Set up a mass oscillating on the end of a spring (a mass-spring oscillator).

(a)   **Describe, by sketching a graph, how the amplitude of the oscillating mass changes with time.**

(b)   **What function might describe how the amplitude decreases with time?**

(c)   **What are the forces causing the damping?**

 Problem   How does the amplitude of the mass-spring oscillator decay with time?

Set up a model

Consider a mass of m kilograms oscillating vertically on the end of a spring with spring constant k newtons per metre and natural length l metres. Assume that there is a damping force, R newtons, proportional to the speed of the mass and acting in the opposite direction to the motion.

Let e metres be the extension of the spring when the mass is in equilibrium and x metres be the displacement from equilibrium at time t seconds.

Analyse the problem

When the mass is in static equilibrium, $R = 0$. By Hooke's law:

$$T = mg$$
$$\Rightarrow k\,e = mg$$

The damping force R is of the form:

$$R = Cv$$

where v ms^{-1} is the speed of the mass and C is a constant, the **damping coefficient**.

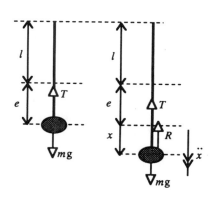

> **Using Newton's second law, show that the equation of motion for the mass is:**
>
> $$m\ddot{x} + C\dot{x} + kx = 0$$

This is the equation for **damped SHM**. The solutions for this equation are considered on Tasksheet 3.

TASKSHEET 3 – *Damped SHM*

There are three possible types of solution to the damped SHM equation:

$$m\ddot{x} + C\dot{x} + kx = 0$$

according to the values of *m*, *C* and *k* . They are:

- **overdamping**   when $C^2 > 4mk$;
- **critical damping**   when $C^2 = 4mk$;
- **underdamping**   when $C^2 < 4mk$.

$C^2 > 4mk$

The auxiliary equation has real roots. The mass does not complete an oscillation.

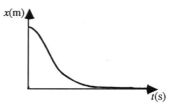

$C^2 = 4mk$

The auxiliary equation has equal roots. As in the case of overdamping the mass does not complete an oscillation. In this situation the amplitude decays to zero most rapidly.

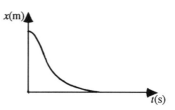

$C^2 < 4mk$

The auxiliary equation has imaginary roots. The mass oscillates with decaying amplitude.

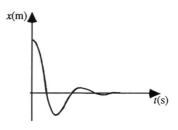

Example 2

The differential equation describing the motion of a shock absorbing device of mass m kilograms is

$$m\ddot{x} + 18\dot{x} + 3x = 0$$

Find the mass for which the system is critically damped.

Solution

The auxiliary equation is $mp^2 + 18p + 3 = 0$

$$\Rightarrow p = \frac{-18 \pm \sqrt{(324 - 12m)}}{2m}$$

For critical damping, the auxiliary equation must have equal roots, i.e. $324 = 12m$.

The system is critically damped when the mass is 27 kg.

Exercise 2   (Take g = 10 ms^{-2}.)

1.   A mass on the end of a spring performs damped harmonic motion given by:

$$x = 0.2\, e^{-0.5t}\, \sin 2t$$

where x metres is the displacement of the mass at time t seconds.

Sketch a graph of displacement against time for $0 < t < 8$ and interpret the graph.

2.   A clock has a simple pendulum of length 20 cm with a bob of mass 180 grams. The air resistance force on the bob is of magnitude $3.6k$ times its speed.

(a)   Draw a diagram showing the forces acting on the bob and indicating the direction of motion.

(b)   Show that the differential equation for the motion of the bob, swinging freely with small amplitude, is:

$$\ddot{\theta} + 20k\, \dot{\theta} + 50\, \theta = 0$$

where θ is the small angular displacement of the pendulum from the downward vertical.

(c)   Find the condition on k for the pendulum to oscillate with underdamped harmonic motion.

3. A particle of mass 5 kg is suspended from a fixed support by means of a light spring, of natural length 1.6 metres and spring constant 45 Nm^{-1}, so that it hangs vertically.

(a) Find the equilibrium position of the particle below the support.

The particle is projected downwards, from equilibrium, with a speed of 2 ms^{-1}. When moving with speed v ms^{-1} vertically, the motion is resisted by a damping force of magnitude $30v$ newtons.

(b) If x metres is the displacement of the particle below the equilibrium position at time t seconds, write down a differential equation in x and t to describe the particle's motion.

(c) Show that the motion is critically damped and find x in terms of t.

4E. A Hookean spring of natural length 0.5 metre is used in a simple set of scales to measure the weights of objects placed on the pan. The pan of mass 0.5 kg rests on top of the spring and causes it to compress by 2 cm.

(a) Find the value of the spring constant k .

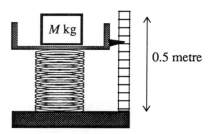

(b) A block of mass M kg is placed on the pan causing the spring to oscillate. There is a damping force $R = 10v$ newtons, where v ms^{-1} is the speed of the pan. The equation of motion for the subsequent damped oscillations is:

$$(M + 0.5)\ddot{x} + 10\dot{x} + kx = 0$$

Show that the general solution to the differential equation is of the form:

$$x = A_0 e^{-\frac{10t}{2M+1}} \cos(nt + \varepsilon)$$

where A_0 is the initial amplitude.

Hence find an expression for n in terms of M.

(c) Find, in terms of M, the time taken for the system to settle down to oscillations of only 25% of the initial amplitude.

(d) What effect would removing the damping force have on the system?

5.3   Forced oscillations

After its opening in July 1940, it was noticed that the Tacoma Narrows bridge, Washington, USA, oscillated in the wind.   Taking a ride on the bridge became a popular attraction. The fun did not last long. In November 1940 the wind was strong, forcing the bridge to oscillate with increasing amplitude. After a few hours the strain on the structure was too great. The bridge began cracking and finally collapsed.

(a)   **Consider a child on a swing being pushed.**

    (i)   **For the best effect, when should you push the swing?**

    (ii)   **What would happen if you pushed a little earlier or later?**

(b)   **Take a spring loaded with a few masses and try pulling upwards periodically to set up a forced oscillation. When should you apply a force to increase the amplitude?**

In these examples, the key point to note is that to produce oscillations the force must be applied repeatedly at regular intervals in the direction of motion. So the force, F , is dependent on time.

One way to model the external driving force is as a periodic function, for example $F = F_0 \cos pt$, where F_0 is its amplitude.

Consider the following experiment to investigate forced oscillations. A mass-spring oscillator is attached by a string to a peg on a rotating turntable.

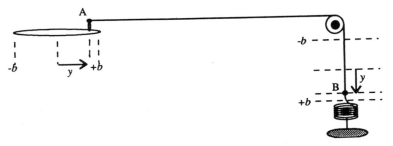

As the peg at A rotates it causes the end B of the string, attached to the top of the spring, to move up and down. If the peg is fixed at a distance of b metres from the centre of a turntable, then the displacement, y metres, of the end of the string at B is in the range $-b \le y \le +b$. Let the turntable rotate with constant speed p rad s^{-1}. If the radius b is very small compared with the length AB, then the displacement, y, can be approximated by $y = b \cos pt$.

Problem   How does the rate of rotation of the peg affect the oscillations of the mass on the end of the spring?

Set up a model

Consider a spring of length l metres and spring constant k Nm^{-1} attached to the string at B.

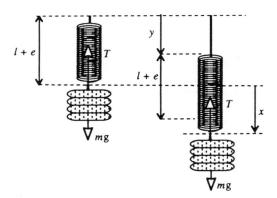

You can assume that:

- the spring obeys Hooke's law for the whole of the motion;
- air resistance is negligible;
- friction in the pulley can be ignored (i.e. assume there are no damping forces);
- the mass on the spring is a particle of mass m kg;
- the extension of the spring is e metres when the mass is in equilibrium;
- the displacement of the mass from the equilibrium position is x metres at time t;
- the displacement of the top of the spring is y metres where $y = b \cos pt$.

80

(a) Show that the tension, T, in the spring is:

$$T = k\,(e + x - y)$$

(b) Using Newton's second law, show that:

$$\ddot{x} + \omega^2 x = b\omega^2 \cos pt, \text{ where } \omega^2 = \frac{k}{m}$$

This is an example of an equation for **forced SHM**. The solution of this equation is the sum of a complementary function, which is the solution to the SHM equation $\ddot{x} + \omega^2 x = 0$, and a particular integral.

For $p \neq \omega$, show that a particular integral is:

$$x = \frac{b\omega^2}{\omega^2 - p^2} \cos pt$$

Hence the general solution to the equation for forced oscillations is:

$$x = A \cos(\omega t + \varepsilon) + \frac{b\omega^2}{\omega^2 - p^2} \cos pt, \text{ if } p \neq \omega$$

Interpret/validate

This solution for the forced oscillation is the sum of two terms, the first representing the unforced oscillation of natural angular frequency, ω, and the second term having the angular frequency of the driving force, p. The graph shows an oscillation where $\omega = 8p$.

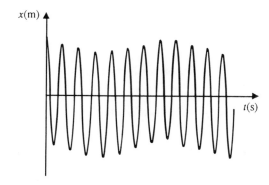

The graph shows the combination of the two oscillations. The curve oscillates with a period of approximately 1 second for the unforced oscillation. The peaks of the curve oscillate with a longer period of about 8 seconds, the time period of the driving force.

(a) Describe the effect of changing the angular frequency of the driving force.

(b) Show that if $p = \omega$ the particular integral is:

$$x = \frac{b\omega}{2} t \sin \omega t$$

When $p = \omega$, the amplitude of the forced oscillations tends to infinity. This situation is known as **resonance**. The graph shows resonance when $A = 0$, $b = 0.25$ and $\omega = 6$.

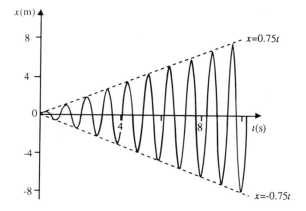

The mass oscillates with increasing amplitude. It seems as if the amplitude will continue to grow, but in reality this is unlikely. At some point the spring would either overstretch and break, or it would not be able to compress to less than its natural length. There is also likely to be damping in the system due to air resistance or friction, and this would restrict the increase in amplitude.

The equation of motion for forced simple harmonic motion is of the form:

$$\frac{d^2 x}{dt^2} + \omega^2 x = F(t)$$

The general solution is the sum of a particular integral and a complementary function (with two arbitrary constants).

Exercise 3

1. (a) Given that $x = t \cos \omega t$ is a particular integral of an equation of motion for oscillations:

$$\ddot{x} + \omega^2 x = F(t)$$

find $F(t)$.

   (b) Sketch the graph of displacement against time and interpret it.

2. The equation of motion of a particle at the end of a flag pole oscillating from side to side on a windy day is given by:

$$\frac{d^2 x}{dt^2} + 100x = 200 \cos pt$$

where p rad s^{-1} is the frequency of the gusts of wind and x metres is the horizontal displacement of the end of the flag pole.

   (a) Find the value of p for which resonance occurs.

   (b) By substitution, or otherwise, show that the displacement of the particle when resonance occurs is given by $x = 0.05 \cos 10t + 10t \sin 10t$, where 0.05 metre is the initial displacement when the particle is at rest.

   (c) Sketch the graph of the displacement for $0 \le t \le 5$ seconds.

   (d) Interpret the result and comment on its validity.

3. A baby of mass 12 kg is bouncing up and down in her baby-bouncer. She uses her legs to apply an upward force at the lowest point of each bounce. The oscillations are modelled by the equation:

$$12\ddot{x} + 108x = 60 \sin 3t$$

where x metres is the displacement of her centre of gravity from its equilibrium position.

   (a) Give two assumptions used to set up this model.

   (b) Find the angular frequency of the unforced oscillations.

   (c) Describe the subsequent motion of the baby and comment on the validity of the model.

5.4   Modelling oscillations

There are many situations that can be modelled using the theory contained in Chapters 4 and 5.

> **All the situations in the picture involve oscillations that can be modelled as either simple harmonic, damped or forced oscillations.**
>
> **What problems involving oscillations can you think of for each situation? What assumptions would you make to model the situations?**

From one of these situations you may find a problem that is suitable for an extended investigation. It should involve modelling with differential equations and it may be possible to validate your solutions by devising a simple practical simulation or by obtaining real data. Note that the differential equations you set up may have very complicated analytical solutions, in which case you should attempt to obtain as accurate a numerical solution as possible.

After working through this chapter you should:

1. be able to recognise the damped and forced SHM equations and be able to find solutions by an appropriate method;

2. be able to set up a model for an oscillating body and apply Newton's second law to obtain equations as appropriate for:

   • damped SHM,

   • forced SHM;

3. be able to interpret solutions graphically and analytically with reference to amplitude, frequency and time period;

4. be able to sketch graphs of displacement, velocity and acceleration against time for an oscillating body;

5. understand what is meant by the terms overdamped, critically damped and underdamped;

6. understand what is meant by resonance;

7. appreciate the advantages and limitations of a numerical solution as compared with an analytical solution.

Pendulum clocks

Problem Investigate how the time period of oscillation of a simple pendulum is affected by varying:

- the mass, *m* kilograms of the bob,
- the length, *l* metres of the pendulum,
- the initial angle of displacement, α radians.

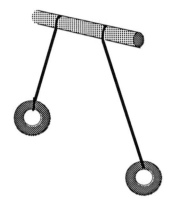

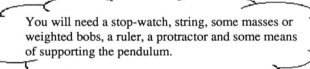

You will need a stop-watch, string, some masses or weighted bobs, a ruler, a protractor and some means of supporting the pendulum.

1. Set up a simple pendulum and begin by making some qualitative observations of the effects that changing each of the variables, *m*, *l* and α, have on the time period of oscillation.

    (Hint: You might try comparing the time period for a pendulum with a very heavy bob with that of a medium or light weight bob, or a long pendulum with a short one, etc.)

2. Choose one of the variables *m*, *l* or α, and set up an experiment to collect more detailed data.

3. By plotting a graph of the results, or otherwise, suggest a relationship between the time period and your chosen variable.

Calculating acceleration

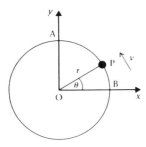

A particle moves in a circle of radius r.

At time t, its speed is v and angle POB $= \theta$.

Its angular speed is the rate of change of θ, $\dfrac{d\theta}{dt}$ or $\dot{\theta}$.

1. Show that $\begin{bmatrix} \cos\theta \\ \sin\theta \end{bmatrix}$ is a unit vector in the direction $\overrightarrow{OP}$.

2. With respect to the (x, y) axes shown in the diagram, the displacement $\overrightarrow{OP}$ is given by:

$$\mathbf{r} = r \begin{bmatrix} \cos\theta \\ \sin\theta \end{bmatrix}$$

Find the velocity $\mathbf{v}$ and show that its magnitude is $r\dot{\theta}$.

3. (a) Show that the acceleration is given by:

$$\mathbf{a} = -r\dot{\theta}^2 \begin{bmatrix} \cos\theta \\ \sin\theta \end{bmatrix} + r\ddot{\theta} \begin{bmatrix} -\sin\theta \\ \cos\theta \end{bmatrix}$$

   (b) Show that $\begin{bmatrix} -\sin\theta \\ \cos\theta \end{bmatrix}$ is a unit vector in a direction perpendicular to $\overrightarrow{OP}$.

   (Hint: Use the scalar product.)

Thus the acceleration has two components:

$r\dot{\theta}^2$ radially inwards ;

$r\ddot{\theta}$ tangentially in the direction of increasing θ.

Damped SHM

OTHER OSCILLATIONS

TASKSHEET 3

In the following questions consider a mass of m kilograms oscillating on the end of a spring with spring constant $k = 10$ Nm^{-1}, with a damping coefficient $C = 20$ Nm^{-1}s. The mass is released from rest with an initial displacement of 2 metres.

The equation of motion for damped simple harmonic motion is:

$$m\ddot{x} + C\dot{x} + kx = 0$$

1.   Obtain the auxiliary equation by making the substitution $x = Ae^{pt}$.

2.   The auxiliary equation has two roots:

$$p_1 = \frac{-C + \sqrt{(C^2 - 4mk)}}{2m} \quad \text{and} \quad p_2 = \frac{-C - \sqrt{(C^2 - 4mk)}}{2m}$$

Using the given values of k and C, show that there are three possible cases, giving a condition on the size of the mass for each case.

CASE 1:   If p_1 and p_2 are both real, then the general solution is $x = Ae^{p_1 t} + Be^{p_2 t}$, where A and B are arbitrary constants.

3.   Find the solution for a mass of 7.5 kg on the end of the spring. Sketch the graph of displacement against time and describe the motion of the mass.

In this case the motion is said to be **overdamped**.

CASE 2:   If $p_1 = p_2$, then the general solution is $x = (A + Bt)\,e^{-\frac{Ct}{2m}}$, where A and B are arbitrary constants.

4.   Find the solution for a mass of 10 kg on the end of the spring. Sketch the graph of displacement against time and describe the motion of the mass.

In this case the motion is said to be **critically damped**.

CASE 3:   If p_1 and p_2 are imaginary, then the general solution:

$$x = Ae^{-\frac{Ct}{2m}}\cos(nt + \varepsilon)$$

where $n = \frac{\sqrt{(4mk - C^2)}}{2m}$ and A and ε are arbitrary constants.

5.   Find the solution for a mass of 100 kg on the end of the spring. Sketch the graph of displacement against time and describe the motion of the mass.

In this case the motion is said to be **underdamped**.

6.   In the underdamped case, the general solution has an oscillating factor, $\cos(nt + \varepsilon)$ and a decay factor, $e^{-\frac{Ct}{2m}}$. Describe what happens to the motion as $C \to 0$.

1.   The usual model for the motion of a simple pendulum of length l metres in a gravitational field of strength g newtons per kilogram gives the time period T seconds as:

$$T = 2\pi \sqrt{\left(\frac{l}{g}\right)}$$

A particular pendulum clock is designed to have a period of 1 second at the surface of the Earth, where g = 9.81.

(a)   Calculate the time period for the same clock on the surface of the Moon, where g = 1.62.

(b)   Why is this result for the time period likely to be more consistent on the Moon than on the Earth?

2.   The motion of a harp's string is modelled by the function $x = ae^{-t} \cos \omega t$, where x metres is the displacement of the centre of the string from its equilibrium position.

For a string which is initially released from a displacement of 1 cm and which vibrates 100 times a second:

(a)   calculate a and ω;

(b)   show that x satisfies the damped SHM equation, $\ddot{x} + 2\dot{x} + (\omega^2 + 1) x = 0$.

3.   The vibration of part of the harp's sounding board is modelled by a forced SHM equation,

$$\ddot{x} + \omega^2 \dot{x} = a \cos \omega t$$

where a is a small constant, ω is the angular frequency of the string's vibration, and x metres is the displacement of a particular point on the board about its mean position.

(a)   Show that $x = \frac{at}{2\omega} \sin \omega t$ is a particular solution.

(b)   Sketch the graph of this solution and interpret it.

4.   (a)   Give a reason why you might use a numerical method to solve the equation of motion of a pendulum:

$$\ddot{\theta} = -\frac{g}{l} \sin \theta$$

(b)   Give two disadvantages of numerical solutions compared with algebraic solutions.

SOLUTIONS

1 *Modelling resisted motion*

1.1 Introduction

> **(a)** In what situations can resistance be used to advantage?
>
> **(b)** What can be done to minimise the drag in cases where it is undesirable?

(a) Air resistance restricts the speed of movement through air. In parachuting, this air resistance is used to reduce speed sufficiently to enable a person to land safely.

Air resistance plays an important role in many sports. Its effect on a badminton shuttlecock is especially easy to observe. A sky-diver can alter her speed significantly either by curling up her body or by falling in a spread-eagled position.

(b) Drag can be minimised by keeping speeds low. In cases where this is impractical it can be reduced by aerodynamically-shaping (streamlining) objects and smoothing their surfaces.

Exercise 1

1. (a) A sky-diver free-falling.

    (b) The person and the rhinoceros using parachutes. The parachute has such a large cross-sectional area that the models for air resistance would have virtually the same value for k.

2. Assume that resistance is proportional to surface area.

    For A: surface area = 8 m^2

resistance = $16v$ newtons

    For B: surface area = 2 m^2

resistance = $4v$ newtons

3. Though the cross-sectional areas are the same, the shape of the object affects the resistance to motion. The cone falling point first is more aerodynamic and would experience a smaller resistance to motion.

1.3   Modelling a sky-diver's descent

> (a)   Model the sky-diver with a force diagram.
>
> (b)   Assume that her terminal speed is 50 ms^{-1} and that air resistance is modelled by the force $R = Kv$. Hence deduce the value of K.
>
> (c)   Show how Newton's second law can be used to obtain the differential equation of motion:
> $$\frac{dv}{dt} = 10 - 0.2v$$

(a)

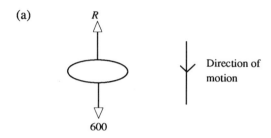

(b)   By Newton's second law:

$$600 - Kv = 60\frac{dv}{dt}$$

At terminal speed, $\frac{dv}{dt} = 0$ $\Rightarrow 600 = K \times 50$
$\Rightarrow K = 12$

(c)   Substituting K into the equation of motion:

$$600 - 12v = 60\frac{dv}{dt}$$
$$\Rightarrow \quad 10 - \frac{12}{60}v = \frac{dv}{dt}$$
$$\Rightarrow \quad \frac{dv}{dt} = 10 - 0.2v$$

> **Sketch and interpret solutions which pass through the points:**
>
> (a)   (5, 0)
> (b)   (0, 10)
> (c)   (0, 50)
> (d)   (0, 60)
>
> **Think of some real situations which would have these initial conditions.**

(a)

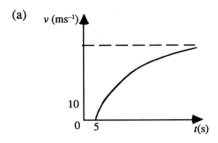

At time $t = 5$, the sky-diver has zero speed. This could be a second sky-diver, falling after a 5 second delay. The motion is the same as the first sky-diver.

(b)

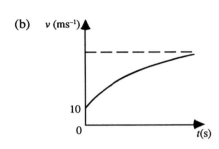

At $t = 0$, the sky-diver is moving at 10 ms^{-1} downwards.
She may have been ejected from the aeroplane at 10 ms^{-1} and reaches terminal speed more quickly.

(c)

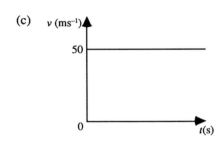

At $t = 0$, the sky-diver is moving at 50 ms^{-1}.
The sky-diver is already at terminal speed and will remain at this speed.

(d)

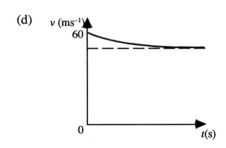

At $t = 0$, the sky-diver is moving at 60 ms^{-1}, which is 10 ms^{-1} faster than terminal speed.
She quickly slows down to the new terminal speed of 50 ms^{-1}. Previously she may have been free-falling in a more aerodynamic position.

Exercise 2

1. (a)

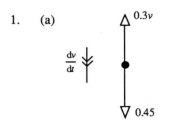

By Newton's second law:

$$0.45 - 0.3v = 0.045 \frac{dv}{dt}$$

$$\Rightarrow 10 - \frac{300}{45}v = \frac{dv}{dt}$$

$$\Rightarrow \frac{dv}{dt} = 10 - \frac{20}{3}v$$

(b)

Time $t_{n+1} = t_n + 0.01$	Speed $v_{n+1} = v_n + 0.01a_n$	Acceleration $a_{n+1} = 10 - \frac{20}{3}v_n$	Height $h_{n+1} = h_n - 0.01v_n$
0	0	10	12
0.01	0.1	10.0	12.0
0.02	0.2	9.3	12.0
0.03	0.3	8.7	12.0
0.04	0.4	8.0	12.0
...	...	...	...
8.13	1.5	0.0	0.015
8.14	1.5	0.0	0.000
8.15	1.5	0.0	−0.015

The time taken for the mouse to fall 12 metres is approximately 8.14 seconds.

(c)   The mouse's speed on impact is 1.5 ms^{-1}.

(d) $dt = 0.005$ gives a time of 8.145 seconds;
$dt = 0.001$ gives a time of 8.149 seconds.

(Note that if you assumed the mouse falls with constant speed of 1.5 ms^{-1}, this would give a time of fall of 8 seconds.)

2.   (a)

(b)   At maximum speed, $9K = 180 \Rightarrow K = 20$

(c)   By Newton's second law:

$$180 - 20v = 60\frac{dv}{dt}$$

$$\Rightarrow \quad 9 - v = 3\frac{dv}{dt}$$

3.   (a)   The main assumptions are:

- the skier is a particle;
- the resistance is modelled as $R = kv^2$;
- the gradient of slope is constant.

(b)   At terminal speed, $\frac{dv}{dt} = 0 \Rightarrow 65g \sin 20° - 0.5v^2 = 0$

$$\Rightarrow v \approx 21$$

The terminal speed is 21 ms^{-1} (76 km h^{-1}).

4. (a)

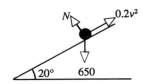

By Newton's second law along the slope:

$$650 \sin 20° - 0.2v^2 = 65\frac{dv}{dt}$$

At terminal speed, $\quad 0.2v^2 = 650 \sin 20°$
$$\Rightarrow v = 33.3$$

The new terminal speed is 33.3 ms^{-1} (approximately 120 kmh^{-1}).

(b) Use a step-by-step method with $a = 10 \sin 20° - \frac{v^2}{325}$, $v + a\,dt \rightarrow v$ and $h + v\,dt \rightarrow h$.

A step size of 0.1 gives $h = 2500$ at time 81.8 seconds.

1.4   Terminal speed

> **Two models for the resistance force have been suggested:**
> $$R = Kv \text{ and } R = kv^2$$
>
> **Given a terminal speed of w metres per second, show that these models lead respectively to the following expressions for w:**
> $$w = \frac{mg}{K} \text{ and } w = \sqrt{\left(\frac{mg}{k}\right)}$$

$R = Kv$

At terminal speed, $mg = Kw \Rightarrow w = \frac{mg}{K}$

$R = kv^2$

At terminal speed, $mg = kw^2 \Rightarrow w^2 = \frac{mg}{k}$
$$\Rightarrow w = \sqrt{\left(\frac{mg}{k}\right)}$$

(a) Interpret the expressions $w = \frac{mg}{K}$ and $w = \sqrt{\left(\frac{mg}{k}\right)}$.

(b) Explain how a sky-diver is able to change terminal speed during the free-fall.

(c) Why is the sky-diver's terminal speed much slower once the parachute is opened?

(d) Would the sky-diver have the same terminal speed on the Moon?

(e) Explain why, when two or more sky-divers link up in free-fall, their terminal speed does not increase significantly .

(a) The terminal speed increases with mass and gravity but decreases as K or k increases. If the model is $R = Kv$, then mass is directly proportional to the terminal speed. However, if the model is $R = kv^2$, then the rate of change of terminal speed decreases as mass increases.

For a mouse, a small increase in mass, for example 10 grams, will have a large effect on its terminal speed. A similar increase in a sky-diver's mass has very little effect on her terminal speed.

(b) A sky-diver can change her terminal speed by altering her position as she falls, so that more or less surface area is presented to the oncoming air, and by making her shape more aerodynamic. These adjustments would alter the value of k in the resistance model.

(c) The parachute has a much greater area than the sky-diver, so that k is much greater. A large value of k, with m and g unchanged, results in a slower terminal speed.

(d) On the Moon, gravity is less than on Earth. However, there is no air on the Moon so k is approximately zero in the model. Hence the terminal speed is very large.

(e) When two sky-divers link up, the resulting 'body' has double the mass and double the surface area. Since $\frac{m}{k}$ remains constant there should be no change in terminal speed.

Exercise 3

1.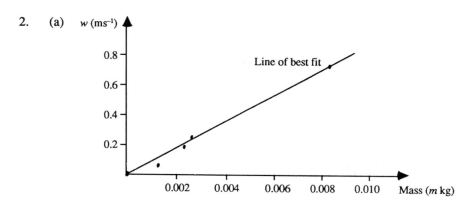

$R \approx 0.005v^2$

2. (a)

w (ms⁻¹) axis label: $w \ (\text{ms}^{-1})$

Line of best fit

Mass (m kg)

(b) $w = 85\,m$ seems to fit the data best. This suggests that the most appropriate model is $R = Kv$.

(c)   At terminal speed, $mg = Kw \Rightarrow w = \dfrac{g}{K}\,m$

$$\Rightarrow \frac{g}{K} = 85$$

$$\Rightarrow K \approx 0.118$$

3. (a)   2 A4 sheets: Double the mass, the same area.
                                            Terminal speed = $2w$.

(b)   A3 sheet: Double the mass, double the area.
                                            Terminal speed = w.

(c) $\frac{1}{2}$ A4 sheet: Half the mass, half the area.
                                            Terminal speed = w.

(d)   Folded A4 sheet: The same mass, half the area.
                                            Terminal speed = $2w$.

In practice, the sheets do not fall vertically but glide from side to side and are tilted at an angle to the horizontal. The results above are therefore only rough approximations to what would happen.

1.5   Another force – upthrust

> **(a)**   **Describe how the upthrust on the airship might vary as it rises to the stratosphere.**
>
> **(b)**   **Why is the upthrust due to air negligible for a cannon-ball, but significant for a child's helium balloon?**

(a)   Upthrust depends on the volume of the airship, the density of air and the value of g. Assuming the airship has a fixed envelope of gas and is not an inflatable or hot air balloon, then the volume would remain reasonably constant. (If this were not the case the volume would increase as the pressure of the surrounding air decreased.) As the airship rises, the surrounding air becomes considerably less dense. The stratosphere is about 18 km above the Earth's surface, so the gravitational attraction will be only slightly smaller than near the surface. The result will be that the upthrust force will decrease as the airship rises, and at some point will equal the weight of the airship.

(b)   The upthrust is equal to the weight of air displaced. The density of a cannon-ball made of iron is approximately 8000 kg m^{-3} which is over 6000 times denser than the displaced air. Thus the upthrust is about $\frac{1}{6000}$ of the weight of the cannon-ball and can be ignored.

The density of helium in the balloon is approximately 0.18 kg m^{-3}. The weight of the displaced air is greater than the combined weight of the balloon and the helium inside it, so the upthrust force is greater than the weight and cannot be ignored.

Exercise 4

1.   (a)   Volume of sphere, $V = \frac{4\pi}{3} \times (0.1)^3 = \frac{4}{3}\pi \times \frac{1}{1000}$ m^3

Weight of lead sphere $= 11\,000V\,g = \frac{440}{3}\pi$ newtons

Weight of iron sphere $= 8000V\,g = \frac{320}{3}\pi$ newtons

Weight of water displaced $= 1000V\,g = \frac{40}{3}\pi$ newtons

$$W - R - U = m\frac{dv}{dt}$$

Lead sphere: $\frac{440}{3}\pi - 16v - \frac{40}{3}\pi = \frac{44}{3}\pi\frac{dv}{dt}$

$\Rightarrow \quad \frac{400}{3}\pi - 16v = \frac{44}{3}\pi\frac{dv}{dt}$

Iron sphere: $\frac{320}{3}\pi - 16v - \frac{40}{3}\pi = \frac{32}{3}\pi\frac{dv}{dt}$

$\Rightarrow \quad \frac{280}{3}\pi - 16v = \frac{32}{3}\pi\frac{dv}{dt}$

(b)   At terminal speed, $\frac{dv}{dt} = 0$

Lead sphere: $\frac{400}{3}\pi = 16v \Rightarrow v = 26.18$

The terminal speed is 26.18 ms^{-1}.

Iron sphere: $\frac{280}{3}\pi = 16v \Rightarrow v = 18.33$

The terminal speed is 18.33 ms^{-1}.

2.   Assume that your body can be approximated to a cylinder.

For example:

Volume = height x area of cross–section

         = 1.70 x π x 0.12 x 0.12

         = 0.077 m^3

(a)   0.077 x 10 x 1.29 ≈ 1 newton

(b)   When you are floating you are in equilibrium, so the upthrust force is equal to your weight. For example, if your mass is 60 kg, then the upthrust is 600 newtons.

(c)   0.077 x 10 x 1000 = 770 newtons

3.   (a) $U = 2200$ x 10 x 1.29 = 28 380 newtons

(b)

$$U - W - R = m\frac{dv}{dt}$$

$$\Rightarrow 820 - R = 2756\frac{dv}{dt}$$

Initially the balloon is at rest, so the air resistance $R = 0$.

$$\Rightarrow \frac{dv}{dt} = \frac{820}{2756} = 0.2975$$

The initial acceleration is 0.3 ms^{-2} upwards.

(c)   As the balloon rises, the resistance will increase. Eventually the resistance force and weight of the balloon will equal the upthrust. The balloon will continue to rise with constant speed. (The upthrust will decrease as the balloon rises and the density of air decreases and so the balloon will eventually reach an equilibrium height.)

2   *Analytical methods*

2.1   Motion at 'low' speeds

Exercise 1

1.   (a)   The forces are upthrust, weight and air resistance.

By Newton's second law:

$$U - W - R = m \frac{dv}{dt}$$

$$U - 0.2 - 0.5v = 0.02 \frac{dv}{dt}$$

The upthrust force is 1.2 N.

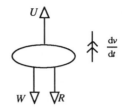

(b) $\frac{dv}{dt} = 0 \Rightarrow 1 - 0.5v = 0$

The terminal speed is 2 ms^{-1}.

2.   (a)

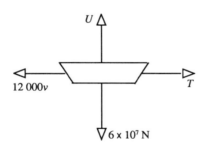

U is the upthrust.

T is the tension in the cable.

(b)   At a constant speed, $T = 12\ 000v$

When $v = 1.5$, the tension in the cable is 18 000 N.

3.   (a)

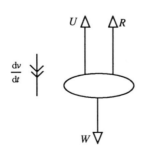

By Newton's second law:

$$W - R - U = m \frac{dv}{dt}$$

$$\Rightarrow 1.1 - 0.7v - 0.12 = 0.11 \frac{dv}{dt}$$

$$\Rightarrow \qquad \frac{dv}{dt} = \frac{98 - 70v}{11}$$

(b) $\frac{dv}{dt} = 0 \Rightarrow v = 1.4$. The terminal speed is 1.4 ms^{-1}.

(c)

$$\int_0^v \frac{1}{98-70v}\, dv = \int_0^t \frac{1}{11}\, dt$$

$$\Rightarrow \quad \ln\left|\frac{98-70v}{98}\right| = -\frac{70}{11}t$$

$$\Rightarrow \qquad v = 1.4\left(1 - e^{-\frac{70}{11}t}\right)$$

Integrating again,

$$x = \int_0^t 1.4\left(1 - e^{-\frac{70}{11}t}\right) dt = 1.4\left(t + \frac{11}{70}e^{-\frac{70}{11}t} - \frac{11}{70}\right)$$

Using a graphical calculator, the value of t for which $x = 12$ can be found to be approximately 8.7. The chick therefore takes 8.7 seconds to fall to the ground.

4. (a)

By Newton's second law:

$$0.06 - 0.05v = 0.006\frac{dv}{dt}$$

$$\Rightarrow \frac{dv}{dt} = \frac{10}{6}(6 - 5v)$$

$$\int_0^v \frac{1}{6-5v}\, dv = \int_0^t \frac{10}{6}\, dt$$

$$\Rightarrow -\frac{1}{5}\ln\left|\frac{6-5v}{6}\right| = \frac{10t}{6}$$

$$\Rightarrow v = 1.2\left(1 - e^{-\frac{25}{3}t}\right)$$

As $t \to +\infty$, $v \to 1.2$.

The terminal speed of the feather is 1.2 ms^{-1}.

(b) $1 - e^{-\frac{25}{3}t} = 0.99$

$$\Rightarrow t = 0.5526$$

The time taken is 0.55 seconds.

(c) **For the marble:** $30 = \frac{1}{2} \times 10 \times t^2$

The marble takes 2.45 seconds.

For the feather: $x = \int_0^t 1.2 \left(1 - e^{-\frac{25}{3}t} \right)$

$$x = 1.2 \left(t + \frac{3}{25} e^{-\frac{25}{3}t} - \frac{3}{25} \right)$$

In the first 0.55 second the feather falls 0.52 metre. The feather falls the remaining distance at approximately 1.2 ms^{-1} and so the time taken to fall 30 metres is:

$$0.55 + \frac{30 - 0.52}{1.2} = 25.12 \text{ seconds}$$

(d) The speed of the marble on impact is 24.5 ms^{-1}.

The speed of the feather on impact is its terminal speed, 1.2 ms^{-1}.

2.2 Motion at 'high' speed

(a) **Show that** $\dfrac{1}{2w} \ln \left| \dfrac{w-v}{w+v} \right| = -\dfrac{gt}{w^2}$

(b) **Hence show that** $v = w \left(\dfrac{1 - e^{-\frac{2gt}{w}}}{1 + e^{-\frac{2gt}{w}}} \right)$

(a) From tables of standard integrals, $\displaystyle\int_0^v \frac{1}{v^2 - w^2}\, dv = \left[\frac{1}{2w} \ln \left| \frac{v-w}{v+w} \right| \right]_0^v$

$$= \frac{1}{2w} \ln \left| \frac{w-v}{w+v} \right|$$

Whereas, $\displaystyle\int_0^t \frac{-g}{w^2}\, dt = -\frac{gt}{w^2}$

(b) $\qquad -\dfrac{2gt}{w} = \ln \left| \dfrac{w-v}{w+v} \right|$

Then $\dfrac{w-v}{w+v} = e^{-\frac{2gt}{w}} \Rightarrow w - v = (w+v) e^{-\frac{2gt}{w}}$

$$\Rightarrow \quad w \left(1 - e^{-\frac{2gt}{w}} \right) = v \left(1 + e^{-\frac{2gt}{w}} \right)$$

$$\Rightarrow v = w \left(\frac{1 - e^{-\frac{2gt}{w}}}{1 + e^{-\frac{2gt}{w}}} \right)$$

Sketch the graph of speed against time for the sky-diver where $w = 50$ and $g = 10$.

Verify that $v \to w$ as $t \to +\infty$.

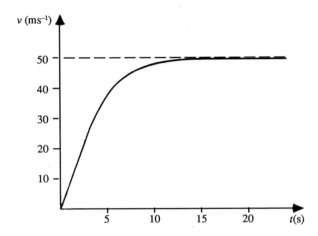

From the graph, as $t \to +\infty$ then $v \to 50 = w$

From the expression $v = w \dfrac{\left(1 - e^{-\frac{2gt}{w}}\right)}{\left(1 + e^{-\frac{2gt}{w}}\right)}$, $v \to w$ because $e^{-\frac{2gt}{w}} \to 0$.

Exercise 2

1. (a) $-1 - 0.0025v^2 = 0.1v \dfrac{dv}{dx}$

   $\Rightarrow -400 - v^2 = 40v \dfrac{dv}{dx}$

   $\displaystyle\int_{12}^{0} \dfrac{40v}{400 + v^2}\, dv = \int_{1}^{H} -1\, dx$

   $\Rightarrow \left[\dfrac{40}{2} \ln (400 + v^2)\right]_{12}^{0} = -H + 1$

   The maximum height is 7.15 metres.

   (b)   When $R = 0$, $144 = 2g\,(H - 1) \Rightarrow H = 8.2$

   The air resistance reduces the maximum height by more than a metre.

104

2. (a) $-\lambda v^2 = 1200 \dfrac{dv}{dt} \Rightarrow \dfrac{dv}{dt} = -\dfrac{\lambda}{1200} v^2$

(b) Separating variables, $\displaystyle\int_{30}^{v} \dfrac{1}{v^2} \, dv = \int_{0}^{t} -\dfrac{\lambda}{1200} \, dt$

$$\left[-\dfrac{1}{v} \right]_{30}^{v} = \left[-\dfrac{\lambda t}{1200} \right]_{0}^{t} \Rightarrow v = \dfrac{1200}{\lambda t + 40}$$

(c) Substituting $t = 5$, $v = 10$: $10 = \dfrac{1200}{40 + 5\lambda} \Rightarrow \lambda = 16$

For speed $v = 5$: $5 = \dfrac{1200}{40 + 16t} \Rightarrow t = 12.5$

The boat takes 12.5 seconds to slow down to 5 ms⁻¹.

3. (a) By Newton's second law:

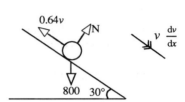

$$800 \sin 30° - 0.64v^2 = 80v \dfrac{dv}{dx}$$
$$\Rightarrow v \dfrac{dv}{dx} = 5 - 0.008v^2$$

Separating variables:

$$\int_{0}^{v} \dfrac{v}{5 - 0.008v^2} \, dv = \int_{0}^{85} 1 \, dx$$

$$\Rightarrow \dfrac{-1}{0.016} \left[\ln (5 - 0.008v^2) \right]_{0}^{v} = 85$$

$$\Rightarrow v = 21.55$$

The speed of the jumper at the end of the ramp is 21.6 ms⁻¹.

(b) As the jumper leaves the ramp the skis tilt and the area presented to the oncoming air increases. The air resistance is likely to increase.

4. (a) By Newton's second law:

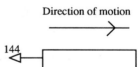

Direction of motion

$$-36v^2 - 144 = 1800 \dfrac{dv}{dt} \Rightarrow \dfrac{dv}{dt} = \dfrac{-(4 + v^2)}{50}$$

(b) Separating variables:

$$\int_{28}^{0} \dfrac{1}{4 + v^2} \, dv = \int_{0}^{t} -\dfrac{1}{50} \, dt$$

$$\Rightarrow \left[\dfrac{1}{2} \tan^{-1} \left(\dfrac{v}{2} \right) \right]_{28}^{0} = \left[-\dfrac{1}{50} t \right]_{0}^{t}$$

$$\Rightarrow t = 37.49$$

The time taken to free-wheel to rest is 37.5 seconds.

2.3   Modelling resisted motion

> **All the situations in the picture above could be modelled using the differential equations in this chapter. What problems does the picture suggest that you could investigate? What assumptions should you make in each case?**

The following suggestions are just some examples of the assumptions which would be needed to set up simple models for the situations depicted. In most cases a simple practical experiment can be devised to simulate and validate your solutions.

High diver

The problem could be one of determining the depth of the pool required for diving platforms of different heights, or you might look at the speed of entry to the water for different types of dives, for example, a swallow dive, a pike dive, a tuck dive. There are two parts to the motion of the diver, the fall through air and the motion in the water. Your assumptions may include statements about:

- the deceleration at the point of entry to the water;
- the posture of the diver's body;
- the models for the resistance force in air and water;
- the terminal speed of the diver in air and in water;
- the upthrust force acting on the diver in the water;

...

Cars at traffic lights

The problem you could consider is the effect streamlining has on reducing the drag on a vehicle and hence its maximum speed. Your assumptions may include statements about:

- the driving force in each car;
- the mass of each car;

...

A suggestion for a practical is to investigate the streamlining of plasticine shapes falling through a liquid, where the terminal speeds are slower and thus measurable.

Meteorology balloons

These balloons are used to measure the pressure, density and temperature of the atmosphere. When released, they travel upwards reaching a maximum height. You might try to investigate how high a balloon might rise. Both the upward motion and the motion near to the maximum height can be modelled. For the balloon to stop, the upthrust acting on it must decrease as it rises until it is equal to the weight of the balloon. The decrease in the upthrust is principally due to the air becoming less dense. (Note however, that as the pressure decreases the volume of the balloon will increase.)

Your assumptions may include statements about:

- the variation of gravity over the distance travelled by the balloon;
- the volume of the balloon;
- the variation in density of air with height;

...

Lorry on an escape lane

The problem may be to find the length of the escape lane required for lorries travelling at different speeds or for lorries of different masses. If the brakes fail to slow the lorry on the incline then it can be steered into a gravel or sand filled lane, where the extra resistance force will halt the vehicle. Possible assumptions concern:

- the initial speed of the lorry;
- the escape lane;
- the model of the resistance when the lorry slides in the gravel or sand ;

...

Shuttlecock

You could compare the maximum range and path of a shuttlecock with that of an unresisted projectile. The problem may be to discover if 45° is still the angle of projection required to achieve maximum range. This is an example of resisted motion in two dimensions. One way to model the motion is to consider the resistance force in component form, for example:

$$R = -\begin{bmatrix} ku \\ kv \end{bmatrix} \text{ newtons, where } \begin{bmatrix} u \\ v \end{bmatrix} \text{ ms}^{-1} \text{ is the velocity of the shuttlecock.}$$

The motion can be analysed numerically and graphically using the step-by-step method. The position of the shuttlecock can be plotted at various times to give its overall path. Possible assumptions might define:

- the height of projection;
- the initial velocity of the shuttlecock;
- the terminal speed of the shuttlecock;

...

Diver floating up

Divers who surface too rapidly after spending some time at depths greater than 3 metres can be subject to decompression sickness, known as the bends. Since heavier divers will rise more slowly the problem could be to determine the extra weight a diver should carry to avoid rising too quickly. You could consult a decompression table in an encyclopaedia to find out the decompression procedure for a diver rising from various depths. Your assumptions may include statements about:

- the upthrust on the diver;
- the posture of the diver;
- the maximum safe speed of the diver;

...

3 Variable mass and weight

3.1 The Moon-lander

> (a) Solve the problems using the assumptions above.
>
> (b) Which of the assumptions would you want to change in order to obtain more realistic solutions?

(a)

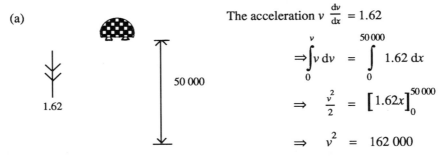

The acceleration $v \frac{dv}{dx} = 1.62$

$$\Rightarrow \int_0^v v \, dv = \int_0^{50\,000} 1.62 \, dx$$

$$\Rightarrow \frac{v^2}{2} = \left[1.62x \right]_0^{50\,000}$$

$$\Rightarrow v^2 = 162\,000$$

The impact speed v is 402.5 ms^{-1}.

To obtain the time to impact, integrate $\frac{d^2x}{dt^2} = 1.62$ with respect to t, twice.
Then $50\,000 = \frac{1}{2} 1.62t^2 \Rightarrow t = 248.5$

The time until impact is 248.5 seconds.

(b) In the model, the only assumption likely to change is that the gravitational attraction does not remain constant for the whole motion. It is smaller at 50 km from the Moon and increases as the lander gets nearer the surface. Thus the initial acceleration is smaller, and increases as the lander falls.

> Interpret these graphs, suggesting which model of gravity is more appropriate for the motion over the ranges shown.

(a) From 0 to 2000 metres there is little variation in g_h. Over this range it is reasonable to assume that g_h is a constant equal to the gravitational acceleration at the surface (i.e. 1.62 ms^{-2} for the Moon).

(b) From 0 to 200 000 metres there is a small but noticeable decrease in g_h. It almost seems to be decreasing linearly with height over this range. For motion between the surface and a lunar orbit you might model gravity as a linear function.

(c) From 0 to 20 000 000 metres the acceleration due to the force of gravity begins to diminish noticeably. At 20 000 km away, $g_h = 0.35$ ms^{-2} and will eventually become negligible as the height tends to infinity. For journeys over this range gravity should be modelled using Newton's law of gravitation.

3.2 Escaping from the Earth

> **(a)** Using a graph plotter, sketch the graph of U as a function of H for appropriate values of G, M and R.
>
> **(b)** Confirm that the value of the asymptote is $U = \sqrt{\left(\frac{2GM}{R}\right)}$.
>
> **(c)** What is significant about the asymptote?

(a) For the Moon, $G = 6.67 \times 10^{-11}$, $M = 7.35 \times 10^{22}$ and $R = 1.74 \times 10^6$.

The graph of U against H is:

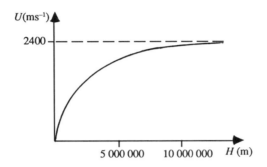

(b) The asymptote gives the value of U at which the maximum height reached by the projectile tends to infinity. Hence the asymptote is at the speed at which the projectile escapes.

(c) From the graph, the asymptote for the values of G, M and R given above is around $U = 2400$ which is approximately $\sqrt{\left(\frac{2GM}{R}\right)}$ for the Moon.

> **Calculate the escape speed from the surface of the Earth and comment on the validity of this value.**

Using $G = 6.67 \times 10^{-11}$, $M = 5.98 \times 10^{24}$ and $R = 6.378 \times 10^6$ in the formula gives the escape speed from the Earth as $11\ 184$ ms^{-1}.

It was assumed that air resistance was negligible in setting up the model. However, travelling through Earth's atmosphere the air resistance would slow the projectile considerably. This would suggest that a greater speed of projection is required to escape.

In the text at the start of this section, the speed of the rocket at cut-off is given as 35 579 feet per second, which is approximately 10 800 ms^{-1}. This is comparable to the solution, although it is less than you might expect. In setting up the model it was assumed that the attraction of other bodies is negligible, but as you move further away from the Earth, the Moon's attraction becomes more significant. Furthermore, at cut-off the rocket is already at a height of 180 miles (288 km) above the Earth's surface so it would not need as great a speed to escape from this point.

Exercise 1

1.   (a)   Since G is a universal constant, the escape speed, $U \propto \sqrt{\left(\dfrac{M}{R}\right)}$.

           U is greater for a planet of the same mass but smaller radius.

   (b)   Skylab has a mass of only 70 000 kg. If you were any distance greater than a few centimetres from the centre of mass then your escape speed would be extremely small. It would be wise for astronauts to secure themselves with a safety cable when on the outside of space stations in deep space.

2.   Let M be the mass and R the radius of the Earth. Using Newton's second law towards the Earth:

$$mv \frac{dv}{dx} = \frac{GMm}{(R + 3\,000\,000 - x)^2}$$

$$\int_{10}^{v} v\,dv = \int_{0}^{3 \times 10^6} \frac{GM\,dx}{(R + 3\,000\,000 - x)^2} = \left[\frac{GM}{(R + 3\,000\,000 - x)} \right]_{0}^{3 \times 10^6}$$

$$\Rightarrow \frac{1}{2}v^2 - 50 = \frac{GM}{R} - \frac{GM}{R + 3\,000\,000}$$

Substituting $R = 6.378 \times 10^6$ and $M = 5.98 \times 10^{24}$ gives $v = 6325.5$.

The impact speed of the meteor is 6325 ms^{-1} (approximately 22 770 km h^{-1}).

3.   (a)

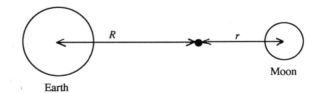

           Earth   Moon

         Let $d = 3.84 \times 10^8$ m represent the distance between the Earth and the Moon. Let R metres be the distance from the Earth of the position where the resultant gravitational attraction is zero and r metres be the distance from the Moon.

         Therefore $\dfrac{GE}{R^2} = \dfrac{GM}{r^2}$, where E is the mass of the Earth and M is the mass of the Moon.

110

Substituting $r = d - R$:

$$\frac{E}{R^2} = \frac{M}{(d-R)^2}$$

$$\Rightarrow d - R = R\sqrt{\left(\frac{M}{E}\right)}$$

$$\Rightarrow R = \frac{d}{1 + \sqrt{\left(\frac{M}{E}\right)}}$$

Substituting in values for d, M and E gives $R = 3.46 \times 10^8$.

The gravitational attraction of Earth equals that of the Moon at 3.46×10^8 metres from the centre of the Earth.

(b)   The craft slows down as it moves away from the Earth until it passes through this point and then begins to accelerate towards the Moon.

4.   (a)   Using Newton's second law towards the meteor:

$$mv\,\frac{dv}{dx} = \frac{G \times 1 \times 10^{14}\, x\, m}{(17 + 449 - x)^2}$$

Separating variables, where U is the impact speed:

$$\int_0^U v\,dv = \int_0^{449} \frac{6670}{(466 - x)^2}\,dx$$

$$\Rightarrow \tfrac{1}{2}U^2 = \left[\frac{6670}{(466 - x)}\right]_0^{449} = \frac{6670}{17} - \frac{6670}{466}$$

$$\Rightarrow U^2 = 756$$

$$\Rightarrow U = 27.5$$

The impact speed of the probe is 27.5 ms^{-1}.

(b)   The equation of motion for the probe was:

$$v\,\frac{dv}{dh} = -\frac{G \times 1 \times 10^{14}}{(17 + h)^2}$$

Integrating gives:

$$\tfrac{1}{2}v^2 - \tfrac{1}{2}V^2 = 6670\left(\frac{1}{17 + h} - \frac{1}{42}\right)$$

where V is the escape speed required.

To escape, $v > 0$ as $h \to \infty$, so $\tfrac{1}{2}V^2 \geq \frac{6670}{42} \Rightarrow V \geq 17.82$

In order to escape, the probe should have been travelling faster than 17.82 ms^{-1} when it reached 25 metres.

5E. To estimate your jump speed, U ms^{-1}, you could find the maximum height, H metres, you can jump off the Earth's surface and use the formula $U = \sqrt{(2gH)}$. Typical values for U would be between 2 ms^{-1} and 4 ms^{-1}.

If the asteroid is assumed to be a sphere of radius R and density D then its mass is $M = \frac{4}{3}\pi R^3 D$. You can therefore escape if

$$U \geq \sqrt{\left(\frac{2GM}{R}\right)} = \sqrt{\left(\frac{8}{3}\pi R^2 DG\right)}$$

The maximum radius is $R = \sqrt{\left(\frac{3U^2}{8\pi DG}\right)}$

For an asteroid of the same density as the Earth (i.e. $D = 5520$ kgm^{-3}) the maximum radius is $R = 569.4U$.

For jumping speeds in the range $2 < U < 4$ this gives asteroids that one could jump off with radii in the range 1139 metres $< R < 2278$ metres.

There are known asteroids in the solar system with radii between 1000 and 2000 metres but their mass is not known. It is feasible that you could land on a small asteroid, walk around carefully and jump off.

An asteroid smaller than 1 km radius would be difficult to stay on whereas it would be safe to walk on one with a radius greater than 2.5 km even though your weight would be very small.

3.3 Rocket propulsion

> Show that if $v = 0$ when $t = 0$, then
>
> $$v = C \ln \left| \frac{M_0}{M_0 - \mu t} \right|. \quad \text{Interpret this solution.}$$

The equation of motion of the rocket is $(M_0 - \mu t)\frac{dv}{dt} - \mu C = 0.$

Separating variables:

$$\int_0^v dv = \int_0^t \frac{\mu C}{M_0 - \mu t}\, dt$$

$$\Rightarrow v = \mu C \left[-\frac{1}{\mu} \ln | M_0 - \mu t | \right]_0^t$$

$$\Rightarrow v = C \ln \left| \frac{M_0}{M_0 - \mu t} \right|$$

The rocket's speed increases from zero, the acceleration increasing as the burnt fuel is ejected.

When $t = \dfrac{M_0}{\mu}$, the speed of the rocket tends to infinity.

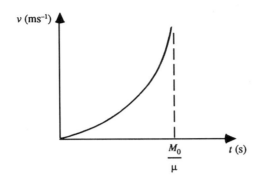

If the rate at which the fuel is ejected, μ, is doubled then the time before the fuel runs out is halved. Hence, though the rocket would accelerate at a different rate its final speed would be the same. The final speed of the rocket would increase if the speed at which the fuel is ejected, C, is increased.

Exercise 2

1.   At $t = 20$, the mass becomes zero and v becomes infinite. In reality this does not happen because the fuel runs out before this, leaving the astronaut moving at constant speed.

2.   At time t: At time $t + dt$:

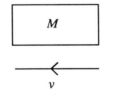
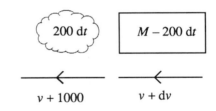

(a)   Applying conservation of momentum:

$$Mv = (M - 200\,dt)(v + dv) + 200\,dt\,(v + 1000)$$

$\Rightarrow$ $0 = M\,dv + 1000 \times 200\,dt$, since the $dv\,dt$ term is negligible

$\Rightarrow M\dfrac{dv}{dt} = -200\,000$

(b)   At time t, $M = 9000 - 200t$

$\Rightarrow (9000 - 200t)\dfrac{dv}{dt} = -200\,000$

(c)
$$\int_{250}^{0} dv = \int_{0}^{t} \frac{-2000}{90-2t} \, dt$$

$$\Rightarrow -250 = \frac{2000}{2} \ln |90 - 2t| - \frac{2000}{2} \ln |90|$$

$$\Rightarrow \ln \left| \frac{90-2t}{90} \right| = -\frac{1}{4}$$

$$\Rightarrow 90 - 2t = 90 \, e^{-\frac{1}{4}}$$

$$\Rightarrow t = \frac{90}{2} \left(1 - e^{-\frac{1}{4}}\right) = 9.95$$

The time taken before the spacecraft stops is 9.95 seconds.

3. (a) $M = 10\,000 - 50t$

(b) $M \frac{dv}{dt} = -Mg + 100\,000$

$$\Rightarrow \frac{dv}{dt} = -10 + \frac{100\,000}{10\,000 - 50t}$$

Integrating:

$$v = \left[-10t + \frac{100\,000}{-50} \ln |10\,000 - 50t| \right]_{0}^{180} \approx 2805$$

After 3 minutes the rocket is travelling at 2805 ms^{-1} approximately.

4. (a) Assumptions are:

- gravity is constant at 9.8 ms^{-2};
- air resistance is modelled by $R = kv^2$ newtons;
- the rate and speed of the fuel ejection is constant;
- there are no other external forces, such as attraction from other bodies;
- upthrust is negligible.

(b) Possible reasons are:

- as the rocket ascends into the upper atmosphere and beyond the air resistance will decrease;
- gravity will decrease as the rocket moves away from the Earth;
- the rocket may not continue to travel vertically upwards;
- there may be discontinuities in the change of M due to 'stages' of the rocket being ejected;
- the fuel may be ejected at a different rate or speed as the rocket travels further away from the Earth.

5. The lander takes off when

$$\mu C \geq M g_M$$

i.e. $180 \times 150 \geq (1.8 \times 10^4 - 180t) \, g_M$

The lander takes off after 7.4 seconds.

3.4   Varying mass

(a)   How does the rate of ascent of the balloon change as sand, used as ballast, is poured over the side?

(b)   Describe the possible motion of the trolley on the slope if the bucket of water is leaking.

(c)   What happens to the motion of the masses in the 'Bricklayer's lament' if a heavy chain is used instead of string?

(a)   The forces acting on the balloon are its weight, upthrust and air resistance. If the balloon is ascending, then either there is a resultant force acting upwards or the balloon is in dynamic equilibrium such that the upthrust equals the weight and air resistance.

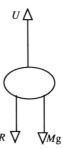

As sand is poured out of the balloon the mass of the balloon decreases and the resultant upward force increases. The balloon will accelerate upwards, and if there were no air resistance then the rate of acceleration would increase as the mass of the balloon decreased. However the faster the balloon ascends the greater the force resisting the motion, so the balloon will eventually approach a constant speed upwards. This speed will be greater since the balloon is getting lighter.

(b)   If the bucket of water is heavier than the trolley there will be a resultant force on the trolley acting up the incline. The trolley will accelerate up the slope. As the water leaks from the bucket, the resultant force will decrease and so the rate of acceleration will decrease. At some point the bucket and the trolley may be in equilibrium and the acceleration will be zero. After this the trolley will start to decelerate, stop and then begin to move down the slope, accelerating at an increasing rate. This assumes that, initially, there is the right amount of water in the bucket. Once all the water is gone, the trolley's acceleration will be constant.

(c)   As the chain passes over the pulley, the mass on either side varies. If initially one side is heavier, then the mass on this side will accelerate downwards, assuming there is no friction in the pulley. As more of the chain passes over the pulley to this side the weight imbalance will increase and the mass will accelerate more rapidly.

4 Simple harmonic motion

4.1 Vibrations everywhere

> (a) List some examples where vibrations are beneficial, and some where they can be a disadvantage or even destructive.
>
> (b) What features of an oscillation can be measured?

(a)   Except within a vacuum, vibrations always create sound. Sometimes this is useful, as in speech or music, but it can be disturbing as in 'noise'.

The periodic nature of some oscillations, for example as in a pendulum or spring, can be used to keep time in a clock.

Some vibrations are destructive. The constant rattling of machinery can eventually cause fractures. Vibrations caused by the wind, Earth movements or traffic flow can similarly cause cracking and lead to collapse of towers, bridges or other structures.

Unwanted vibrations can be eliminated by employing a 'damping device', to cause the vibrations to die away quickly.

(b)   The main features of an oscillation that can be measured are:

- the size of the oscillation – called the amplitude;

- the time taken for one oscillation – called the time period;

- and the number of oscillations in a given period of time – called the frequency.

Exercise 1

1.   (a)   The seagull moves up and down on the sea. It has a maximum displacement of 0.7 metre and each oscillation takes about 4 seconds.

The amplitude, a, is 0.7 and $\omega = \frac{2\pi}{4}$, so a suitable function is

$$x = 0.7 \sin\left(\frac{\pi}{2} t\right).$$

(b) The centre of the spin-drier vibrates up and down with an increasing amplitude. The amplitude doubles in 0.5 second. The time for one oscillation is approximately 0.26 second and this appears to be constant.

The amplitude, a, increases from 0.01 after 0.05 second to 0.02 after 0.55 second.

The gradient, $\frac{da}{dt}$, is $\frac{0.01}{0.5} = 0.02$ and the intercept is approximately 0.01.

Therefore the amplitude is growing linearly according to $a = 0.02t + 0.01$. ω is $\frac{2\pi}{0.26} = 24.2$.

A suitable function is $x = (0.02t + 0.01) \sin (24.2t)$.

2. (a)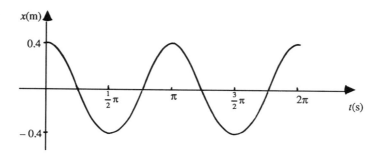

(b) A possible function is $x = 0.4 \cos 2t$.
(Note: The graph represents a simplification of the true motion.)

3. The ruler vibrates quickly. The period is small and the amplitude decreases quickly to virtually zero after one second.

If the initial displacement of the ruler tip is 6 cm, a graph of the displacement against time may be as shown.

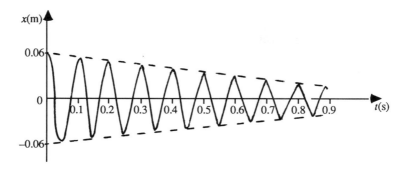

From this graph, the amplitude $a = 0.06 - \frac{0.04}{0.8}t$
$$\Rightarrow \quad a = 0.06 - 0.05t .$$

The period of oscillation is approximately 0.1 second.
So the displacement x is $(0.06 - 0.05t) \cos (20\pi t)$.

4.2   Simple harmonic motion

> **(a)**   Describe how the shadow moves.
>
> **(b)**   Model its displacement with a graph and suggest a suitable function.

(a)   The shadow starts at the edge of the screen, moves to the left and stops after 40 cm. It then begins to move the other way, speeding up as it passes through the centre then slowing to stop 20 cm to the right of the centre. It then moves back, passing through the centre, and repeats the cycle.

(b)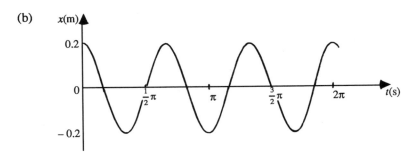

The period of the cycle is $\frac{2\pi}{3}$ seconds and the maximum displacement is 0.2 metre.

The displacement x is $0.2 \cos 3t$.

> **Show that $a \cos (\omega t + \varepsilon)$ is equivalent to $A \cos \omega t + B \sin \omega t$ and express the arbitrary constants A and B in terms of a and ε.**

$$
\begin{aligned}
a \cos (\omega t + \varepsilon) &= a (\cos \omega t \, \cos \varepsilon - \sin \omega t \, \sin \varepsilon) \\
&= (a \cos \varepsilon) \cos \omega t - (a \sin \varepsilon) \sin \omega t
\end{aligned}
$$
So $A = a \cos \varepsilon$ and $B = -a \sin \varepsilon$

Exercise 2

1.   (a)

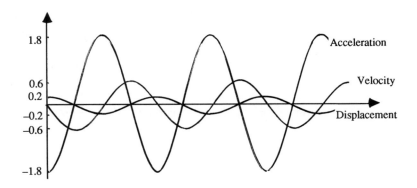

(b) (i)   When the acceleration is zero, the displacement is zero.

(ii) When the acceleration is maximum, the displacement is minimum.

(iii) When the velocity is zero, the displacement is maximum or minimum.

(iv) When the velocity is a maximum, the displacement is zero.

2.
$$x = 0.18 \cos (10.5t)$$
$$\Rightarrow \dot{x} = -0.18 \times 10.5 \sin (10.5t)$$
$$\Rightarrow \ddot{x} = -0.18 \times (10.5)^2 \cos (10.5t)$$
$$\Rightarrow \ddot{x} = -x \times (10.5)^2$$
$$\Rightarrow \ddot{x} + (10.5)^2 x = 0$$

This is the SHM equation, $\ddot{x} + \omega^2 x = 0$, where $\omega = 10.5$.

3. (a) Initial angle, $\varepsilon = \frac{\pi}{2} + 0.8$

$$\Rightarrow x = 0.2 \cos (3t + \frac{\pi}{2} + 0.8)$$

(b) Initial angle $\varepsilon = \pi + 0.8$

$$\Rightarrow x = 0.2 \cos (3t + \pi + 0.8)$$

4.
$$x = A \cos \omega t + B \sin \omega t$$
$$\Rightarrow \dot{x} = -A \omega \sin \omega t + B \omega \cos \omega t$$
$$\Rightarrow \ddot{x} = -A \omega^2 \cos \omega t - B \omega^2 \sin \omega t$$
$$\Rightarrow \ddot{x} = -\omega^2 (A \cos \omega t + B \sin \omega t)$$
$$\Rightarrow \ddot{x} = -\omega^2 x$$
$$\Rightarrow \ddot{x} + \omega^2 x = 0$$

Hence $x = A \cos \omega t + B \sin \omega t$ is a solution to the SHM equation. It is a general solution since it has two arbitrary constants, A and B, corresponding to the two integrations which are required to solve a second order differential equation.

4.3   Modelling an oscillating body

(a) For the baby-bouncer, use the initial conditions $t = 0$, $x = a$ and $\frac{dx}{dt} = 0$ to show that the solution to the differential equation is

$$x = a \cos \sqrt{(\frac{k}{m})} t$$

(b) For $k = 500$, $m = 10$ and $a = 0.6$, sketch the graph of the displacement x against time t for the oscillating baby.

(c) Use the graph to estimate the time period of oscillation.

(a)   The equation of motion is $\ddot{x} = -\omega^2 x$, which has a general solution of the form:

$$x = A \cos(\omega t + \varepsilon)$$

Using the initial condition $x = a$ when $t = 0$ gives $a = A \cos \varepsilon$.

Differentiating the expression for displacement gives $\dot{x} = -A\omega \sin(\omega t + \varepsilon)$.

Initially, $t = 0$, $\dot{x} = 0$ $\Rightarrow$ $0 = -A\omega \sin \varepsilon$ $\Rightarrow$ $\varepsilon = 0$

Hence $a = A \cos 0 = A$

The solution is $x = a \cos(\omega t)$ where $\omega = \sqrt{(\frac{k}{m})}$.

$$\Rightarrow x = a \cos\left(\sqrt{(\frac{k}{m})}\,t\right)$$

(b)

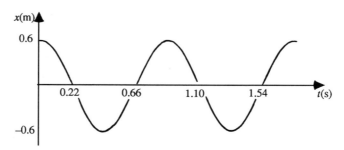

(c)   From the graph the period of one oscillation is 0.88 second. So a baby of mass 10 kg on a spring with a spring constant of 500 Nm⁻¹ will oscillate with a period of just under 1 second.

> **Interpret this formula. What does it tell you about the time period of oscillation for different masses and different strings or springs?**

The time period increases as the mass on the spring increases and the time period is greater for springs with a low spring constant. The oscillations are less rapid for smaller spring constants, k.

Exercise 3

1.   (a)   Displacement, $x = a \cos \omega t$

The initial conditions are $t = 0$, $x = 0.01$

$\Rightarrow 0.01 = a \cos 0 \Rightarrow a = 0.01$

The time period, $T = \dfrac{2\pi}{\omega}$ $\Rightarrow$ $\dfrac{8}{10} = \dfrac{2\pi}{\omega}$

$\Rightarrow \omega = \dfrac{5\pi}{2}$

120

(b)   The displacement of the bob is now $x = 0.01 \cos\left(\frac{5\pi}{2}t\right)$.

$$\Rightarrow \quad \dot{x} = -0.01 \times \frac{5\pi}{2} \sin\left(\frac{5\pi}{2}t\right)$$

So the maximum speed of the bob is $\dot{x} = \frac{5\pi}{200}$.

Differentiating again, $\ddot{x} = -0.01 \times \left(\frac{5\pi}{2}\right)^2 \cos\left(\frac{5\pi t}{2}\right)$

This has a maximum of $\ddot{x} = 0.01 \times \frac{25\pi^2}{4}$.

The maximum speed is $\frac{5\pi}{200} = 0.08$ ms^{-1} and the maximum acceleration is $\frac{25\pi^2}{400} = 0.6$ ms^{-2}.

(c)   When the speed is a maximum, the displacement is zero. When the acceleration is a maximum, the displacement is -0.01 m.

2.   (a)   In equilibrium, $1 = 0.3k$

$$\Rightarrow k = \frac{10}{3}$$

Thus the tension is given by $T = \frac{10}{3}(x + 0.3)$ newtons where x metres is the displacement from the equilibrium position.

(b)

Using Newton's second law downwards:

$$1 - T = 0.1\ddot{x}$$

$$\Rightarrow \quad 1 - \frac{10}{3}(0.3 + x) = 0.1\ddot{x}$$

$$\Rightarrow \quad \frac{-100}{3}x = \ddot{x}$$

So the initial acceleration (when $x = 0.02$) is $\ddot{x} = \frac{-2}{3}$.

The initial acceleration is $\frac{2}{3}$ ms^{-2} upwards.

(c)   The equation of motion for the mass is $\ddot{x} + \frac{100}{3}x = 0$ which is the equation for SHM where $\omega^2 = \frac{100}{3}$.

Hence $\omega = \frac{10}{\sqrt{3}}$ and the time period is given by:

$$\tau = \frac{2\pi}{\omega} = \frac{2\pi\sqrt{3}}{10} = 1.09$$

The time period of the oscillations is 1.09 seconds.

3. (a)

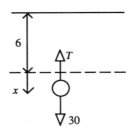

Using Newton's second law downwards:
$$30 - T = 3\ddot{x}$$

From Hooke's law, $T = 15x$.
$$\Rightarrow 30 - 15x = 3\ddot{x}$$
$$\Rightarrow \ddot{x} = 10 - 5x.$$

(b) Try the solution $x = 2 + \cos \sqrt{5}t$
$$\Rightarrow \ddot{x} = -5 \cos \sqrt{5}t$$
$$\Rightarrow 10 - 5x = 10 - 10 - 5 \cos \sqrt{5}t$$
$$= -5 \cos \sqrt{5}t$$
$$= \ddot{x}$$

Therefore $x = 2 + \cos \sqrt{5}t$ is a solution.

(c) The minimum extension of the spring occurs when $x = 2 - 1 = 1$, which is positive.

The string never compresses since the extension is always greater than 1 metre.

4. (a)

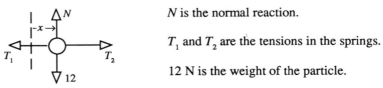

N is the normal reaction.

T_1 and T_2 are the tensions in the springs.

12 N is the weight of the particle.

(b) From Hooke's law, $T_1 = 24x$

and $T_2 = -24x$

Using Newton's second law in the direction of increasing x

$$T_2 - T_1 = 1.2\ddot{x}$$
$$\Rightarrow -24x - 24x = 1.2\ddot{x}$$
$$\Rightarrow -40x = \ddot{x}$$
$$\Rightarrow \ddot{x} + 40x = 0$$

This is the SHM equation where $\omega^2 = 40 \Rightarrow \omega = 6.32$.

The particle performs SHM with angular frequency of 6.32 rad s^{-1}.

5 *Other oscillations*

5.1 The pendulum

> **Explain how you should vary *l* to correct a pendulum clock which runs fast or slow.**

The time period is $\tau = 2\pi \sqrt{(\frac{l}{g})}$ and so $\tau \propto \sqrt{l}$. To increase the time period you should therefore increase the length of the pendulum. If a clock is running fast then the time period is too short so *l* must be increased. If the clock is running slow, then the time period is too long and *l* needs shortening. Your results from Tasksheet 1 should validate these conclusions.

> **(a) For $l = 1, g = 10$ and $\alpha = 0.1$, use a time interval of 0.01 to find the time period of the pendulum.**
>
> **(b) Find the time period if α is changed to 1.5.**

(a) Using a program you should find that θ becomes zero at time 0.50 second. The time period is therefore 2.0 seconds, as is predicted by the solution of the SHM equation.

(b) In this case, a quarter of the time period is 0.58 second. Hence the time period is approximately 2.3 seconds. This is significantly greater than the value of 2 seconds predicted by the SHM equation which is only valid for small amplitudes less than about 0.2 radians.

Exercise 1

1. (a) This is SHM with $\omega = \frac{5}{3}$. The general solution is:

   $$\theta = a \cos\left(\frac{5}{3}t + \varepsilon\right)$$

   The initial conditions give the particular solution:

   $$\theta = 0.12 \sin\left(\frac{5}{3}t\right)$$

   (b) $\tau = 2\pi \times \frac{5}{3} \approx 3.77$

   The time period is 3.8 seconds.

   (c) The main assumptions are:
   - the amplitude is small and constant;
   - the mass is a particle;
   - there is no air resistance or damping;
   - the string is light and inextensible.

2. (a) $0.9 = 2\pi \sqrt{(\frac{l}{g})} \Rightarrow l \approx 0.205$

   The pendulum is approximately 0.2 metre long.

   (b) The general solution is:

   $$\theta = a \cos (7t + \varepsilon)$$

   When $t = 0$, $\theta = 0.17$ and $\dot{\theta} = 0$. Therefore:

   $$\theta = 0.17 \cos 7t$$

   $$\Rightarrow \quad \dot{\theta} = -1.2 \sin 7t$$

   The maximum angular speed of the bob is 1.2 rad s^{-1}.

3. (a) Assume that:

   - friction and air resistance are negligible;

   - the oscillations have small amplitude.

   (b)

   Using Newton's second law tangentially:

   $$0.015 \times 0.2 \times \ddot{\theta} = -0.15\,\theta$$

   $$\Rightarrow \quad \ddot{\theta} + 50\,\theta = 0$$

   (c) The time period is $\frac{2\pi}{\sqrt{50}} \approx 0.9$ second.

4. (a) $2\dot{\theta}\ddot{\theta} = \frac{2g}{l}\dot{\theta}(-\sin \theta)$

   $$\Rightarrow \ddot{\theta} = -\frac{g}{l}\sin \theta$$

   $$\Rightarrow \ddot{\theta} + \frac{g}{l}\sin \theta = 0$$

   (b) $\dot{\theta} = \pm\sqrt{(\frac{2g}{l}\cos \theta + C)}$ with $g = 10$ and $l = 1$

   $\dot{\theta} = 0$ when $\theta = \frac{\pi}{2} \Rightarrow C = 0$

   So $\dot{\theta} = \pm\sqrt{(20 \cos \theta)}$

(c) $\dot{\theta} = \sqrt{(20 \cos \theta)} \Rightarrow \int \frac{d\theta}{\sqrt{(20 \cos \theta)}} = \int dt$

The pendulum oscillates from $\theta = \frac{\pi}{2}$ to $\theta = -\frac{\pi}{2}$ and back again, so a quarter of the time period is given by:

$$\int_{0}^{\pi/2} \frac{d\theta}{\sqrt{(20 \cos \theta)}}$$

Using the mid-ordinate rule (to avoid problems at $\theta = \frac{\pi}{2}$) with 100 strips, an approximate value of 2.28 was obtained by using one particular calculator.

The time period for small oscillations is:

$$2\pi \sqrt{\left(\frac{l}{g}\right)} \approx 2$$

so it appears that the time period increases as the amplitude increases. It should be possible to validate this result experimentally.

5.2   Damping

> Using Newton's second law, show that the equation of motion for the mass is:
>
> $$m\ddot{x} + C\dot{x} + kx = 0$$

$$mg - T - R = m\ddot{x}$$

$$\Rightarrow mg - k(e + x) - C\dot{x} = m\ddot{x}$$

$$\Rightarrow m\ddot{x} + C\dot{x} + kx = 0$$

Exercise 2

1.

- The mass is initally struck from rest at its equilibrium position.
- The period of oscillation is π seconds.
- The amplitude is decaying exponentially and has maximum displacement of 0.14 metre after 0.67 second.
- After 8 seconds the oscillations have almost disappeared. There are about $2\frac{1}{2}$ oscillations.

2. (a)

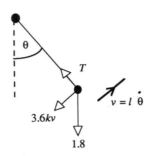

θ

T

$v = l\,\dot\theta$

$3.6kv$

1.8

(b) Using Newton's second law tangentially, in the direction of increasing θ:

$$0.18 \times 0.2 \times \ddot\theta = -1.8\sin\theta - 3.6k \times 0.2\dot\theta$$
$$\Rightarrow \qquad \ddot\theta = -50\sin\theta - 20k\,\dot\theta$$

For small angles, $\theta \approx \sin\theta$:

$$\Rightarrow \ddot\theta + 20k\,\dot\theta + 50\,\theta = 0$$

(c) $p^2 + 20kp + 50 = 0$

$$\Rightarrow p = \frac{-20k \pm \sqrt{(400k^2 - 200)}}{2}$$

It is underdamped if $400k^2 < 200 \Rightarrow k < 0.71$

3. (a)

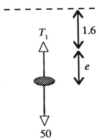

T_1

1.6

e

50

In equilibrium $\quad T_1 = 50$

$$\Rightarrow 45e = 50$$

$$\Rightarrow \quad e = 1.11$$

The equilibrium position is 2.71 metres below the support.

(b)

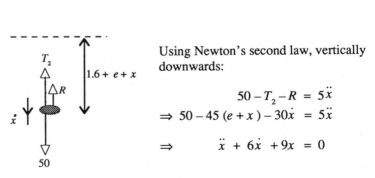

T_2

$1.6 + e + x$

R

$\dot x$

50

Using Newton's second law, vertically downwards:

$$50 - T_2 - R = 5\ddot x$$
$$\Rightarrow 50 - 45\,(e + x) - 30\dot x = 5\ddot x$$

$$\Rightarrow \qquad \ddot x + 6\dot x + 9x = 0$$

(c) $p^2 + 6p + 9 = 0$

$$\Rightarrow p = -3$$

The auxiliary equation has equal roots, hence the motion is critically damped.

$$x = (A + Bt)\, e^{-3t}$$

To satisfy the initial conditions:

$$x = 2t\, e^{-3t}$$

4E (a) Using Hooke's law:

$$5 = 0.02k \quad \Rightarrow \quad k = 250$$

The spring constant is 250 Nm^{-1}.

(b) $(M + 0.5)p^2 + 10p + 250 = 0$

$$\Rightarrow \quad p = \frac{-10 \pm j\,\sqrt{(1000M + 400)}}{2M + 1}$$

$$\Rightarrow \quad x = A_0\, e^{-\frac{10t}{2M+1}} \cos(nt + \varepsilon)$$

where $n = \dfrac{\sqrt{(1000M + 400)}}{2M + 1}$

(c) $e^{-\frac{10t}{2M+1}} = 0.25$

$$\Rightarrow \quad t = \frac{2M + 1}{10}\, \ln 4$$

(d) Removing the damping would mean that the scales would continue to oscillate and would not settle down to allow a reading to be taken.

5.3 Forced oscillations

> (a) Consider a child on a swing being pushed.
>
>   (i) For the best effect, when should you push the swing?
>
>   (ii) What would happen if you pushed a little earlier or later?
>
> (b) Take a spring loaded with a few masses and try pulling upwards periodically to set up a forced oscillation. When should you apply a force to increase the amplitude?

(a) (i)   To increase the amplitude of the swing, the push should be applied at the end of each swing, in the direction in which the swing is about to move.

   (ii)   If the swing were pushed at other times, the effect would not be so great. If it were pushed in the opposite direction to which it was moving, the amplitude would decrease.

(b) This is quite straightforward to test practically. To increase the amplitude, the upward force should be applied when the mass is at its lowest point (i.e. at maximum displacement).

   Note that the effect on the amplitude depends on the frequency with which the force is applied. If this is very much less or very much greater than the frequency of the oscillations then the force will have little effect on the amplitude. The closer the frequencies are, the more the force affects the amplitude, as in (i) above when the frequencies are equal.

(a)   Show that the tension, T, in the spring is:

$$T = k(e + x - y)$$

(b)   Using Newton's second law, show that:

$$\ddot{x} + \omega^2 x = b\omega^2 \cos pt, \text{ where } \omega^2 = \frac{k}{m}$$

(a) Length of spring $= l + e + x - y$

   Extension of spring $= e + x - y$

   $$\Rightarrow \quad T = k(e + x - y)$$

(b) $$mg - T = m\ddot{x}$$

   $$\Rightarrow \quad mg - k(e + x - y) = m\ddot{x}$$

   When in equilibrium, $mg = ke$ and so

   $$-kx + ky = m\ddot{x}$$

   Substituting $y = b \cos pt$:

   $$\Rightarrow \quad m\ddot{x} + kx = kb \cos pt$$

   $$\Rightarrow \quad \ddot{x} + \omega^2 x = b\omega^2 \cos pt$$

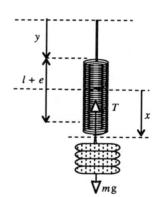

For $p \neq \omega$, show that a particular integral is:

$$x = \frac{b\,\omega^2}{\omega^2 - p^2}\cos pt$$

Try $x = A\cos pt$

$\Rightarrow \quad \ddot{x} = -p^2 A\cos pt$

Substituting in the equation of motion:

$$-p^2 A\cos pt + \omega^2 A\cos pt \equiv b\omega^2\cos pt$$

$$\Rightarrow \quad A = \frac{b\,\omega^2}{\omega^2 - p^2}$$

(a) **Describe the effect of changing the angular frequency of the driving force.**

(b) **Show that if $p = \omega$ the particular integral is:**

$$x = \frac{b\omega}{2}t\,\sin\omega t$$

(a) When the angular frequency of the driving force, p, is very small compared with the angular frequency, ω, of the unforced oscillation, then the amplitude of the forcing term, $\dfrac{b\,\omega^2}{\omega^2 - p^2}$ is approximately equal to b and the time period is very long.

Thus you observe the natural oscillations with only a slight variation in the amplitude.

As p increases for a fixed value of b, the amplitude of the forcing term increases and the time period shortens, hence the variation in the amplitude of the natural oscillation becomes more noticeable. When p is almost equal to ω the variation in amplitude is large. The amplitude of the forced oscillation rises and falls at regular intervals. This phenomenon is known as **beats**. The frequency of the beat is the difference between p and ω.

The graph shows the beats, where $\omega = 3$ and $p = 2.6$.

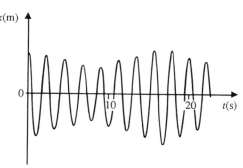

129

At the point where $p = \omega$, the amplitude of the forcing term tends to infinity. The solution is no longer valid since it was obtained on the assumption the $p \neq \omega$. If p is increased further then beats will be obtained once more. As p becomes very large, the amplitude of the forcing tends to zero and has very little effect on the natural oscillation.

(b) $\ddot{x} + \omega^2 x = b\omega^2 \cos \omega t$

Trying $x = At \sin \omega t$:

$2A\omega \cos \omega t - A\omega^2 t \sin \omega t + A\omega^2 t \sin \omega t \equiv b\omega^2 \cos \omega t$

$\Rightarrow \quad A = \dfrac{b\omega}{2}$

Exercise 3

1. (a) $\ddot{x} = -2\omega \sin \omega t - \omega^2 t \cos \omega t$

$\Rightarrow \quad -2\omega \sin \omega t - \omega^2 t \cos \omega t + \omega^2 t \cos \omega t = F(t)$

$\Rightarrow \quad F(t) = -2\omega \sin \omega t$

(b)

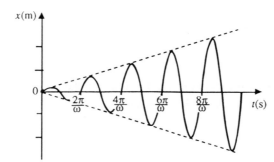

The mass is at rest and is then given an initial velocity. Resonance occurs, the mass oscillating with amplitude growing linearly. The time period is $\dfrac{2\pi}{\omega}$.

2. (a) $\omega = \sqrt{100} = 10$

For resonance, $p = \omega = 10$

(b) $x = 0.05 \cos 10t + 10t \sin 10t$

$\Rightarrow \quad \ddot{x} = 95 \cos 10t + 100 \cos 10t - 1000t \sin 10t.$

Then $\ddot{x} + 100x = 200 \cos 10t$ as required.

When $t = 0$, $x = 0.05$ and $\dot{x} = 0$, satisfying the initial conditions.

130

(c)

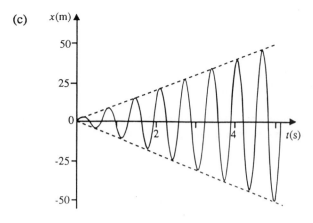

(d) The amplitude of the oscillations is growing linearly. The time period is approximately 0.63 second.

The flag pole would break long before the amplitude reaches 50 m, so the oscillations would not continue after 1 or 2 seconds.

In practice there would be a damping force and the wind is unlikely to blow with consistent strength and frequency.

3.　(a) Some possible assumptions are:

- the upward force is periodic, with angular frequency 3 rad s^{-1};

- the spring is Hookean, where $k = 108$;

- there are no damping forces;

- the baby is a particle.

(b) $\ddot{x} + 9x = 5 \sin 3t$

The angular frequency of the unforced oscillation is 3 rad s^{-1}.

(c) The frequencies of the driving force and unforced oscillation are equal. Hence the baby is resonating and the amplitude of the bouncing will grow.

The model takes no account of the floor or the length of the baby's legs.

5.4 Modelling oscillations

> All the situations in the picture involve oscillations that can be
> modelled as either simple harmonic, damped or forced oscillations.
>
> What problems involving oscillations can you think of for each
> situation? What assumptions would you make to model the situations?

The swing

The motion will vary depending on whether the boy on the swing pumps his legs up and
down, or the child on the ground pushes just once or once every swing. What happens
if the child on the swing is much heavier than the pusher? How will the amplitude of
the swing vary with time?

The likely assumptions might concern:

- the child on the swing;
- air resistance;
- the rope;
- the tree branch swinging or breaking.

For a forced oscillation you could model the push as a periodic force using a
trigonometric function or as a discrete force, $P = 200 \, N$ or $P = 0$ depending on the time.
The latter model would require a numerical method of solution.

The cable car

The cable car would swing if it was very windy. How could you model its motion?
What effect does the angle between the two ropes and the vertical have on the motion?
What happens if the people inside the cable car jump up and down?

You might model the cable car as:

- a particle in the middle of an elastic string oscillating up and down;
- a particle on a light inextensible string swinging from side to side.

It would probably be best, at least at first, to assume the cables are symmetrical about
the vertical. You will have to make an estimate of the mass of the car.

Similar situations are a bird landing on telephone lines, the lights of Blackpool
illuminations strung across the road, or acrobats walking a high wire.

The baby-bouncer

What spring constant is needed for the springs of a baby-bouncer?
How should the motion decay if the baby is not to become motion sick?

You will need to make some assumptions about the average mass of a baby likely to use the bouncer.

Other assumptions may concern the length of her legs when bent or stretched.

Springboards

How does a diving board oscillate with a diver on it?
More interestingly, how does a diver force the oscillation of the board to best effect?

You might make assumptions about:

- the diver's weight;
- the restoring force of the board on the diver;
- air resistance or other damping forces.

Practical measurements could be made of the restoring force at various displacements by hanging weights from the board.

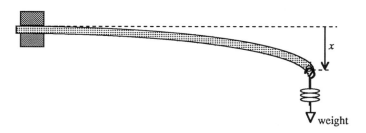

Your first model might be for the situation without damping. This could lead to an equation of motion, and hence to a solution for undamped, unforced oscillations. From practical work a damping term might be hypothesised which would show how the oscillations of the board might decay.

Practical experiments might involve real diving boards or simulations using flexible rulers.

Datasheets

Densities of some fluids (at 0°C, and 1 atmosphere pressure, unless otherwise noted)

Density of dry air at 0°C	1.29 kg m^{-3}
Density of dry air at 20°C	1.20 kg m^{-3}
Density of water at 4°C	1000 kg m^{-3}
Density of sea water at 15°C	1025 kg m^{-3}
Density of helium	0.178 kg m^{-3}
Density of hydrogen	0.0899 kg m^{-3}
Density of olive oil at 15°C	920 kg m^{-3}
Density of crude oil at 15°C	875 kg m^{-3}

Some masses

Ship *Queen Elizabeth*	7.6×10^7 kg
Oil tanker – empty	2.2×10^8 kg
– full	6.6×10^8 kg
Jet airliner (Boeing 747, empty)	1.6×10^5 kg
Skylab	7.0×10^4 kg
Automobile	1.5×10^3 kg

Gravitational constant $G = 6.67 \times 10^{-11}$ Nm^2 kg^{-2}

Earth	Mass	5.98×10^{24} kg
	Radius	6.378×10^6 m
	Mean density	5520 kg m^{-3}
	Gravity at surface	9.81 ms^{-2}
	Period of rotation	23 hrs 56 min 4 sec (8.616×10^4 sec)
	Mean distance from Sun	1.50×10^{11} m
	Period of orbit around Sun	1 year = 365 days 6 hours

Moon	Mass	7.35×10^{22} kg
	Radius	1.74×10^6 m
	Mean density	3340 kg m^{-3}
	Gravity at surface	1.62 ms^{-2}
	Period of rotation	27.3 days
	Mean distance from Earth	3.84×10^8 m
	Period of orbit around Earth	27.3 days

Sun	Mass	1.99×10^{30} kg
	Radius	6.96×10^8 m
	Mean density	1410 kg m^{-3}
	Gravity at surface	274 ms^{-2}
	Period of rotation	26 days (approximately)

The planets in the solar system

Planet	Mean distance from Sun (10^6 km)	Period of revolution (years)	Mass (kg)	Equatorial radius (km)	Surface gravity (g_E)	Period of rotation (days)
Mercury	57.9	0.241	3.30×10^{23}	2 439	0.38	58.6
Venus	108	0.615	4.87×10^{24}	6 052	0.91	243
Earth	150	1.00	5.98×10^{24}	6 378	1.00	0.997
Mars	228	1.88	6.42×10^{23}	3 397	0.38	1.026
Jupiter	778	11.9	1.90×10^{27}	71 398	2.53	0.41
Saturn	1430	29.5	5.67×10^{26}	60 000	1.07	0.43
Uranus	2870	84.0	8.70×10^{25}	25 400	0.92	0.65
Neptune	4500	165	1.03×10^{26}	24 300	1.19	0.77
Pluto	5910	248	6.60×10^{23}	2 500	0.72	6.39

Artificial satellites of the Earth

Satellite	Mass (kg)	Mean distance from centre of Earth (km)	Period (minutes)
Sputnik I	83	6.97×10^3	96.2
Sputnik II	3000	7.33×10^3	104
Explorer I	14	7.83×10^3	115
Vanguard I	1.5	8.68×10^3	134
Explorer III	14	7.91×10^3	116
Sputnik III	1320	7.42×10^3	106

Programs

A straightforward program can be used to analyse the motion of an object in free-fall. An acceleration of $10 - 0.004V^2$ has been assumed in the Euler step programs given below. To adapt the programs to other situations, change the formula for A and check that the expressions for V and H have the correct sign.

Casio graphical calculators

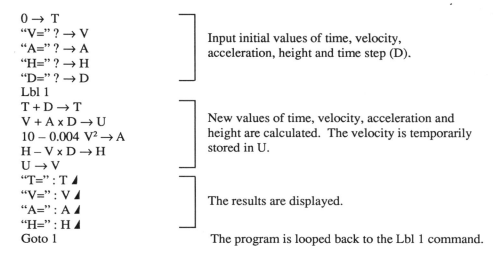

$0 \rightarrow T$
"V=" ? $\rightarrow$ V
"A=" ? $\rightarrow$ A
"H=" ? $\rightarrow$ H
"D=" ? $\rightarrow$ D

Input initial values of time, velocity, acceleration, height and time step (D).

Lbl 1
$T + D \rightarrow T$
$V + A \times D \rightarrow U$
$10 - 0.004 \ V^2 \rightarrow A$
$H - V \times D \rightarrow H$
$U \rightarrow V$

New values of time, velocity, acceleration and height are calculated. The velocity is temporarily stored in U.

"T=" : T ◢
"V=" : V ◢
"A=" : A ◢
"H=" : H ◢

The results are displayed.

Goto 1

The program is looped back to the Lbl 1 command.

- If you do not require all the results to be displayed, then instead of the command of Goto 1, the command:

$$H > 0 \implies Goto \ 1$$

can be put **before** the print instructions. The program will then only display the values of T, V and A when the ground is reached.

- You might also wish to modify the program to print the results at chosen intervals of time, for example every 5 seconds. One suggestions is to input an end time, E:

Lbl 2
"E=" ? $\rightarrow$ E

Insert before Lbl 1.

$T \neq E \implies Goto \ 1$

Insert before the results are displayed.

Goto 2

Replaces Goto 1.

Texas graphical calculators

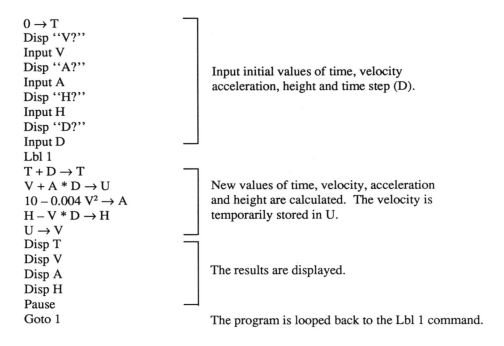

$0 \to T$
Disp "V?"
Input V
Disp "A?"
Input A
Disp "H?"
Input H
Disp "D?"
Input D
                      Input initial values of time, velocity
                      acceleration, height and time step (D).

Lbl 1
$T + D \to T$
$V + A * D \to U$
$10 - 0.004\ V^2 \to A$
$H - V * D \to H$
$U \to V$
                      New values of time, velocity, acceleration
                      and height are calculated. The velocity is
                      temporarily stored in U.

Disp T
Disp V
Disp A
                      The results are displayed.
Disp H
Pause

Goto 1
                      The program is looped back to the Lbl 1 command.

- If you do not require all the results to be displayed, then instead of the command of Goto 1, the commands:

         If $H > 0$
         Goto 1

can be put **before** the print instructions. The program will then only display the values of T, V and A when the ground is reached.

- You might also wish to modify the program to print the results at chosen intervals of time, for example every 5 seconds. One suggestion is to input an end time, E:

                   Lbl 2
                   Disp "E?"   Insert before Lbl 1.
                   Input E
                   If $T \neq E$ Insert before the results are displayed.
                   Goto 1
                   Goto 2   Replaces Goto 1.